John A. Andrew, Benjamin F. Butler

Correspondence between Governor Andrew and Maj.-Gen. Butler

John A. Andrew, Benjamin F. Butler

Correspondence between Governor Andrew and Maj.-Gen. Butler

ISBN/EAN: 9783741124952

Manufactured in Europe, USA, Canada, Australia, Japa

Cover: Foto ©ninafisch / pixelio.de

Manufactured and distributed by brebook publishing software (www.brebook.com)

John A. Andrew, Benjamin F. Butler

Correspondence between Governor Andrew and Maj.-Gen. Butler

BETWEEN

Gov. Andrew and Maj-Gen. Butler.

BOSTON:
PUBLISHED BY JOHN J. DYER,
No. 35 School Street,
1862.

CORRESPONDENCE.

WAR DEPARTMENT, August 10, 1861.

To His Excellency, the Governor of the State of Massachusetts:

General Sherman having been charged with the preparation of an expedition to rendezvous on Long Island, will, on the part of this Department, consult with you as to the troops which can earliest be made available for this service.

Very respectfully, your obedient servant,

THOMAS A. SCOTT, *Acting-Secretary of War.*

WAR DEPARTMENT, August 27, 1861.

To His Excellency JOHN A. ANDREW, *Governor of Massachusetts:*

Sir,—This will be sent you by Brigadier-General Thomas W. Sherman, U. S. Army, who has heretofore communicated with you on the subject of concentrating, in a camp of instruction, a number of regiments of United States Volunteers. As late emergencies may have somewhat interfered with this object, I have now to renew the request that you will put three regiments, as soon as they can be prepared for service, under the orders of General Sherman, who will indicate the place of rendezvous.

I am, Governor, very respectfully,
Your obedient servant,

SIMON CAMERON, *Secretary of War.*

[Telegram.]

WASHINGTON, August 28, 1861.

To Governor ANDREW, *Boston:*

Wardwell authorized to raise a regiment. Cameron to-day orders him to report to you, obeying your instructions. Copy of orders sent you. Secretary promises no more such irregularities. This regiment in addition to five.

C. H. DALTON.

WAR DEPARTMENT, August 28, 1861.

To His Excellency Governor ANDREW, *of Massachusetts, Boston, Mass:*

Sir,—I have the honor to inclose herewith a copy of the Department's letter of this date to Colonel David K. Wardwell, of Boston.

Very respectfully your obedient servant,

JAMES LESLEY, Jr., *Chief Clerk, War Department.*

WAR DEPARTMENT, August 28, 1861.

Colonel DAVID K. WARDWELL, *Boston, Mass:*

Sir,—You will report to his Excellency the Governor of Massachusetts, from whom you will receive instructions and orders in reference to the regiment which this Department has authorized you to raise.

By order of the Secretary of War.

JAMES LESLEY, Jr., *Chief Clerk, War Department.*

EXECUTIVE DEPARTMENT, BOSTON, }
August 28, 1861. }

To Brigadier-General REED, *Quartermaster-General of the Commonwealth.*

General,— * * * * * *

His Excellency desires you, if you find proper occasion to do so, to express the pleasure with which he has this day learned, through a telegram from Washington, that the Secretary of War will not sanction, for the future, any such irregularities with respect to issuing permissions to individuals to raise regiments, as it has permitted itself to sanction during the last few weeks.

It is not an enviable, nor is it an easy task, which the government of this Commonwealth is willing to assume—to take charge of the enlistment and equipment of all regiments which may be required from Massachusetts—but it is essential to the proper organization and comfort of our troops, and to the securing to their families of the legislative provisions for their welfare, that such troops should be enlisted and equipped under its direction, and *therefore* it is willing to assume it.

Until it shows itself incompetent to the task, it is the most efficient and economical agency through which the Federal Government can accomplish its military preparations within the borders of Massachusetts for the volunteer service.

I have the honor to be,
Respectfully, your obedient servant,
A. G. BROWNE, Jr., *Military Secretary.*

Approved, and the Quartermaster-General is requested to confer on the subjects above mentioned with the Military Secretary of the Governor, if he shall be in Washington at the same time.
JOHN A. ANDREW.

WASHINGTON, D. C., September 6, 1861.

To His Excellency Governor ANDREW, *Boston:*

Sir,—The undersigned, having heretofore reported by telegraph and mail concerning other matters embraced in your Excellency's letter of instructions, dated August 28, respectfully submit the following report of our action under the concluding portions of said instructions, relative to the permissions issued by the Federal authorities to individuals to raise regiments in Massachusetts, independently of and conflicting with the regular recruiting system of the Commonwealth.

On the 4th instant, at an interview with the Secretary of War, we repeated to him the substance of that portion of your Excellency's letter, and in reply he assured us of his regret that any such permissions should have been issued heretofore, and of his determination that none should be issued hereafter. He expressed his cordial concurrence with your Excellency's opinion, that the most efficient and economical agency through which the Federal Government can raise regiments in Massachusetts is through the State Government, and seemed fully to appreciate the confusion and conflict of authority which would be caused by the competition of individuals with the regular recruiting system of the State, and the difficulties to which your Excellency might be subjected, in respect to commissioning officers over troops raised under such independent authority. In conclusion, he added that he felt under especial obligation to yourself, and to Massachusetts, for the energy, economy, and honesty with which military affairs had been conducted under your direction.

On the 5th instant, at an interview with the President, we repeated to him the substance of that portion of your Excellency's letter, in the same manner as on the previous day to the Secretary of War, and in reply he stated his concurrence in the opinion that no more independent permissions to raise regiments should be granted to individuals. Without suggestion from ourselves, he spoke of the impossibility of relying upon the States to respond promptly to regular requisitions for troops, if their recruiting system should be harrassed by the competition of individuals engaged in recruiting under independent permissions; but he said such independent permissions as had hitherto been issued had been extorted by the pressure of certain persons, who, if they had been refused, would have accused the government of rejecting the services of so many thousands of imaginary men—a pressure of the persistency of which, no person not subjected to it could conceive. He said that perhaps he had been in error in granting such independent permissions at all, even under this pressure, but that certainly it had not been intended to do any person or any State a wrong. In closing the conversation on this subject, the President added that he was very familiar with it in all its bearings at this moment, because it had been laid before him personally during the few preceding days by His Excellency Governor Morgan, of New York, who, he remarked, appeared to have been embarrassed in the same manner as yourself, but to a greater extent;

that in the instance of New York, an arrangement had, therefore, been made, intended to obviate all these difficulties, and it was to be presumed that it might be necessary to apply the same remedy to the other States.

In this connection we inclose a copy of the General Order of the United States War Department, No. 71, which bears date yesterday, showing the manner in which the subject has been arranged in New York, and we understand the President and Secretary of War to have assured us that the same principles of adjustment are applicable to Massachusetts, and that, if necessary, a similar General Order will be directed to be issued with regard to our own State.

We have the honor to remain,

Respectfully, your obedient servants,

JOHN H. REED, *Quartermaster-General.*
A. G. BROWNE, Jr., *Military Secretary.*

WAR DEPARTMENT, ADJUTANT-GENERAL'S OFFICE,
WASHINGTON, September 5, 1861.

[*General Order, No.* 71.]

I. All persons having received authority to raise volunteer regiments, batteries, or companies, in the State of New York, will immediately report to His Excellency Governor Morgan, at Albany, the present state of their respective organizations. They and their commands are placed under the orders of Governor Morgan, who will re-organize them and prepare them for service in the manner he may judge most advantageous for the interests of the General Government.

By order.

L. THOMAS, *Adjutant-General.*

WAR DEPARTMENT, WASHINGTON, Sept. 5, 1861.

Hon. JOHN A. ANDREW, *Governor of Massachusetts:*

Dear Sir,—In reply to your favor relative to organization of troops, I will say that the best method, in my opinion, is for you to proceed with organization of regiments as authorized, the expense of which will be paid, from time to time, by requisitions from you, accompanied with proper certificates and original bills.

We desire your active co-operation in the organization of an army sufficiently powerful to crush the Southern rebellion and forever set at rest the question of secession.

Allow me to tender the thanks of this Department for the services you have rendered the country by promptly supplying all demands made for forces. Very respectfully, your friend,

SIMON CAMERON, *Secretary of War.*

EXECUTIVE DEPARTMENT, BOSTON, Sept. 7, 1861.

My Dear Sir,—I replied to your favor by telegraph, but have been too busy at work in aid of troops for your movement to write a letter. I have visited General Sherman about it during the past week. We are raising five new regiments *all of which I mean Sherman shall have if you will get an order from the War Department to send them to him.* I hope we shall have most of them recruited this month, if not all of them.

Yours faithfully, JOHN A. ANDREW.

[The above was returned with the following indorsements.]

Respectfully submitted to the War Department.

A. LINCOLN.

September 10, 1861.

Let this be done.

SIMON CAMERON, *Secretary of War.*

I send you the order you desire.

WILLIAM H. SEWARD.

HEAD-QUARTERS U. S. FORCE, NEW YORK, Sept. 9, 1861.

His Excellency JOHN A. ANDREW, *Governor of Massachusetts, Boston:*

Sir,—The public interest requires that the remaining troops for this expedition assemble here at the very earliest day practicable. * * * . * * *

I have the honor to remain your Excellency's most obedient servant,

T. W. SHERMAN, *Brigadier-General commanding.*

WAR DEPARTMENT, Sept. 10, 1861.

Major-General B. F. Butler is hereby authorized to raise, organize, arm, uniform, and equip a volunteer force for the war in the New England States, not exceeding six (6) regiments, of the maximum standard, of such arms and in such proportions and in such manner as he may judge expedient; and for this purpose his orders and requisitions in the Quartermaster, Ordnance, and other Staff Departments of the Army are to be obeyed and anwered, provided the cost of such recruitment, armament, and equipment does not exceed, in the aggregate, that of like troops now or hereafter raised, for the service of the United States.

SIMON CAMERON, *Secretary of War.*

EXECUTIVE DEPARTMENT, BOSTON, Sept. 11, 1861.

Brig.-Gen. THOMAS W. SHERMAN, *New York:*

. General,—His Excellency, Governor Andrew, directs me to say that * * * * the new regiments are going forward towards completion very rapidly. General Wilson has about 900 men in camp to-day, and the other regiments are being recruited in such manner as to give promise of an early filling up of their ranks; so that there is a reasonable prospect of two regiments by the 20th, with three more in a good state of forwardness at that time.

I have the honor to be, your obedient servant,

THOMAS DREW, *Ass't Mil. Sec'y.*

[Telegram.]

WASHINGTON, Sept. 11, 1861.

To Governor ANDREW:

General Butler proposes raising in New England six regiments, to be recruited and commanded by himself and to go on special service.

I shall be glad if you, as Governor of Massachusetts, will answer by telegraph that you consent.

A. LINCOLN, *President.*
SIMON CAMERON, *Sec'y of War.*

[Telegram.]

EXECUTIVE DEPARTMENT, BOSTON, Sept. 11, 1861.

To President LINCOLN, and Sec'y CAMERON, *Washington, D. C.:*

Authorize *State* to raise whatever regiments you wish additional. We will first fulfil engagements with General Sherman ordered by Secretary of War; then add others fast as possible. Will help General Butler to the utmost.

JOHN A. ANDREW, *Governor.*

[Telegram.]

WAR DEPARTMENT, WASHINGTON, Sept. 12, 1861.

To Governor ANDREW, Boston:

Despatch of yesterday received. Massachusetts has done so well in all she has promised, that she shall not be disappointed in any thing she desires from the General Government.

SIMON CAMERON, *Secretary of War.*

NEW YORK, Sept. 11, 1861.

To His Excellency JOHN A. ANDREW, *Governor of Massachusetts, Boston:*

Governor,—The object of my telegram of the 10th was to ascertain if there existed any possibility of being disappointed in the time when the troops would be prepared.

* * * * * * *

I have the honor to remain your most obedient servant,

T. W. SHERMAN, *Brig.-Gen. U. S. A.*

WAR DEPARTMENT, September 12, 1861.

Major-General Butler is authorized to fit out and prepare such troops in New England as he may judge fit for the purpose, to make an expedition along the eastern shore of Virginia *via* the railroad from Wilmington, Delaware, to Salisbury and thence through a portion of Maryland, Accomac, and Northampton Counties of Virginia to Cape Charles.

Transportation agents, quartermasters, and commissaries of subsistence will answer General Butler's requisitions for this purpose.

SIMON CAMERON, *Secretary of War.*

WAR DEPARTMENT, ADJUTANT-GENERAL'S OFFICE,
WASHINGTON, September 16, 1861.
[*General Order, No.* 78.]

I. All persons having received authority from the War Department to raise volunteer regiments, batteries, or companies in the loyal States, are, with their commands, hereby placed under the orders of the Governors of those States, to whom hey will immediately report the present condition of their respective organizations.

These troops will be organized, or re-organized and prepared for service by the Governors of their respective States, in the manner they may judge most advantageous to the interests of the Federal Government.

By order.
L. THOMAS, *Adjutant-General.*

HEAD-QUARTERS, BOSTON, September 23, 1861.
[*General Order, No.* 23.]

Massachusetts has, at present, in active service, sixteen regiments and seven unattached companies of infantry, and one full battery of artillery. There are now in a forward state of organization in the various State camps, the following new regiments and companies:

22d regiment, Colonel Henry Wilson, camp, Lynnfield.
23d " Colonel not designated, camp, Lynnfield.
24th " Colonel Stevenson, camp, Readville.
25th " Colonel Upton, camp, Worcester.
26th " Colonel Jones, camp, Lowell.
27th " Colonel Lee, camp, Springfield.
1st Regiment Cavalry, Colonel not designated, camp, Readville.
1st Battery Artillery, Captain Porter, camp, Cambridge.
3d " Artillery, Captain Follett, camp, Lynnfield.
4th " Artillery, Captain not designated, camp, Lowell.
5th " Artillery, Captain not designated, camp, Lynnfield.

Two more infantry regiments will go into camp in a few days, one of which of is the 28th, to be commanded by Thomas S.

Murphy, and is to form a part of the command of Major-General Butler, whose head-quarters are at Lowell, and the other is the 29th, intended for the Irish (Shields) Brigade, the Colonel of which has not yet been designated.

It is the intention of His Excellency, the Commander-in-Chief, to have these regiments and companies filled to the maximum standard as quickly as possible, and *until they are filled no recruiting except for these regiments and batteries is authorized or can be encouraged by the Commander-in-Chief*, (with the single exception of recruiting to fill vacancies in Massachusetts regiments already in active service,) because it is of the first importance that these organizations should be completed promptly and without delay. The following is an extract from a General Order, issued on the 16th instant, by the Adjutant-General of the United States:

"All persons having received authority from the War Department to raise volunteer regiments, batteries or companies in the loyal States, are, with their commands, hereby placed under the orders of the Governors of those States, to whom they will immediately report the present condition of their respective organizations. These troops will be organized or re-organized and prepared for service by the Governors of the respective States in the manner they may judge most advantageous for the interests of the General Government."

In accordance with the above, *the Commander-in-Chief directs that no new regiments or companies be formed* or ordered into camp, nor any already in camp change their location, *without orders from these head-quarters.*

By command of His Excellency JOHN A. ANDREW, *Governor and Commander-in-Chief.*

WILLIAM SCHOULER, *Adjutant-General.*

[Telegram.]

WAR DEPARTMENT, WASHINGTON, D. C.,
September 23, 1861.

To Governor ANDREW, *Boston:*

Will the three regiments for General Sherman be ready this week? He must be supplied in advance of other applications for same service. Please reply immediately.

SIMON CAMERON, *Sec'y of War.*

[Telegram.]

EXECUTIVE DEPARTMENT, BOSTON, }
September 23, 1861. }

To Hon. SIMON CAMERON, *Sec'y of War, Washington, D. C.:*

I request you not to issue any order detailing any particular Massachusetts regiments to General Butler, but to leave all such details to me. I have pledged certain regiments to General Sherman, and I am determined, if allowed, to keep my word to him. I can provide for Butler otherwise and sufficiently. I shall be obliged if I can receive an answer by telegraph stating that this matter of designating which shall go to Butler and which to Sherman is left to me according to this my request, unless you will now specifically designate which three Sherman shall have; say Wilson's two regiments and the Worcester regiment.

JOHN A. ANDREW, *Governor.*

[Telegram.]

WAR DEPARTMENT, WASHINGTON, }
September 23, 1861. }

To Governor ANDREW:

Select the regiments yourself for Sherman and supply him first.

THOS. A. SCOTT,
Acting Secretary of War.

EXECUTIVE DEPARTMENT, BOSTON, }
September 23, 1861. }

To Major-General BUTLER, *U. S. Volunteers:*

General,—His Excellency Governor Andrew, directs me to mention to you the speedy organization of another Irish Regiment, of which Patrick Donahoe, Esq., acts as *prochein ami*, to be officered, as to its "field," by a list of gentlemen, Messrs. Murphy, Monteith, and Moore, who have been selected after careful consultation. Mr. Donahoe will immediately present a a roster of the other officers of the regiment, for examination and approval. His Excellency would propose to assign this regiment to form part of your command, and would be pleased to hear from you any suggestions concerning a camping ground on which to assemble its recruits. Camp Cameron, at North Cambridge, has been mentioned and favorably received, as its rendezvous, and will be designated as such unless you have desires to the contrary. Your ob't serv't,

     A. G. BROWNE, Jr., *Military Secretary.*

        EXECUTIVE DEPARTMENT, BOSTON,
          September 23, 1861.

To Brig.-General SHERMAN, *U. S. Army:*

 General,—His Excellency Governor Andrew, directs me to write to you that he expects you to exert all the personal effort within your power to secure to your command the contingent which you expect from Massachusetts, and prevent it from being diverted to General Butler or any other officer. His Excellency pledged to you his own personal efforts to secure to you the first regiments whose organization should be completed in the State, after the dispatch to Washington of the five regiments which were forming when you first visited Boston. Those five regiments are all now in the field in active service; and the three which he considers belong rightfully to your command (being the three which will next be completed), are General Wilson's two regiments now encamped at Lynnfield, i. e. the 22d and 23d, and the 25th Regiment now encamped at Worcester. Other regiments can be furnished to General Butler in proper time, and neither he nor any other commanding officer ought to be allowed to divert from you *these* three regiments, which are yours almost by right.

 His Excellency, so far as he can influence the matter, proposes to assign to General Butler the regiment being raised by Col. Jones (the 26th), who is a townsman and personal and political friend of General Butler,—and also an Irish regiment whose organization is in progress. There can be no just pretence on which your claim to the 22d, 23d and 25th can be disputed, but as it is probable that it may nevertheless be drawn in question, His Excellency relies upon you for your own sake to assist him to maintain it. The 22d is already full, and it will be ready to move at the beginning of next week,—certainly by the 1st of October. The 23d and 25th are also in an advanced state of progress.

I have the honor to be, very truly, your ob't serv't,
A. G. BROWNE, Jr.,
Lieut.-Col. and Military Secretary.

HEAD-QUARTERS, CAMP CHASE,
September 24, 1861.

Lt.-Col. A. G. BROWNE, Jr., *Military Secretary:*

Sir,—Your communication of the 23d inst. has been received, in which you speak of the speedy organization of another Irish regiment, and locating a camp therefor.

I would simply say in reply that General Butler has gone to Portland, Me., and I will call his attention to the matter as soon as he returns, which will be to-morrow evening.

I have the honor to be, your ob't serv't,
P. HAGGERTY,
A. A. A. General to Maj. General B. F. Butler.

EXECUTIVE DEPARTMENT, BOSTON,
September 24, 1861.

To Hon. SIMON CAMERON, *Secretary of War, Washington, D. C.:*

Dear Sir,—I have been much perplexed and embarrassed during the last few days by contradictory orders and assurances issuing from your Department, respecting the disposition to be made of the regiments now organizing in this State.

By a recent General Order I am given to understand that the entiredirection of them, until they proceed into active service, is reposed in myself, as the Chief Executive of the Commonwealth. But notwithstanding this Order I find Major-General Butler and Colonel Wilson authorized by authority from your Department to act in some respects more or less independently of me. *For instance, Col. Wilson has to-day received orders from you to report to General Butler, and form a component part of his proposed expedition.* But almost at the same moment I receive from the Assistant Secretary of War a despatch authorizing me to make my own selection of regiments for General Sherman's expedition, and to send them in advance of all others; and under this authorization I shall certainly desire to assign Col. Wilson's regiment to General Sherman, whereas he has previously been ordered by you to report himself otherwise.

I wish to suggest as the most effectual and yet simple method of avoiding such difficulties and embarrassments, that you effect your purposes concerning regiments organizing in this State, *through* and not *outside of* its Governor. I need not say that I have no other ends to subserve except the public advantage, for you are aware that such is the fact without any such assurance; and most assuredly the public advantage can best be subserved, and your own purposes best be accomplished through my agency, so long as the organization of the regiments is entrusted to my control. For I know better than any body else *can* know, the quality of the material of which the troops organizing here are composed. I know their affections, their prejudices, and their desires; and I have been desirous to distribute them among Generals Sherman, Burnside, and Butler, each of whom is of course desirous to secure the best of them, according to my own opinion of the system of distribution which shall most promote their efficiency upon the service for which they are designed.

General Burnside, with most commendable modesty and taste, will, I doubt not from the conversation I have had with him, coincide with my opinions on this subject. But General Butler, it is evident to me, desires naturally to secure to his own command, with or without consultation with me, according as best he may, all the force he can, even to the prejudice of what General Sherman has a positive right to expect from Massachusetts.

I am faithfully and with high regard yours,

JOHN A. ANDREW.

CORRESPONDENCE.

WAR DEPARTMENT, September 27, 1861.

Sir,—Your letter of the 24th instant is received. It is the desire of this Department that General Sherman should be first supplied, and that afterwards General Butler should be furnished with such troops as may be required in aid of his proposed expedition.

It was the intention of this Department to leave to your Excellency all questions concerning the organization of troops in your State, and the Orders to which you refer were designed to be subject to the approval and control of the Executive of Massachusetts.

It will be my endeavor to act strictly in accordance with your suggestions. This Department reposes entire confidence in one who has thus far discharged with fidelity, ability, and energy, every duty required of him by the Federal Government.

I am, with great respect,
Your obedient servant,
SIMON CAMERON, *Secretary of War.*

To His Excellency JOHN A. ANDREW, *Governor of Massachusetts, Boston, Mass.*

NEW YORK, September 27, 1861.

Lt.-Col. A. G. BROWNE, Jr., *Mil. Sec'y of Mass., Boston:*

Dear Sir,—Your favor of the 23d inst. was received yesterday, and the matter was immediately attended to by calling the attention of the Honorable Secretary of War to the subject.

Five regiments are yet waited for, 3 from Mass., 1 from Maine, and 1 from New Hampshire, and it is hoped that they will all be pressed forward at the earliest day.

* * * * * *

Very respectfully, your most ob't,
T. W. SHERMAN, *Brig.-Gen'l commanding.*

WAR DEPARTMENT, October 1, 1861.

To His Excellency JOHN A. ANDREW, *Governor of Massachusetts, Boston, Mass.:*

Sir,—Please send Colonel Stevenson's Regiment when ready for service, to Camp Hempstead, Long Island, with instructions to report to General Burnside for orders.

Yours respectfully,

SIMON CAMERON, *Secretary of War.*

WAR DEPARTMENT, ADJUTANT-GENERAL'S OFFICE,
WASHINGTON, October 1, 1861.

[*General Order. No. 86.*]

I. The six New England States will temporarily constitute a separate military department, to be called the Department of New England. Head-Quarters, Boston. Major-General B. F. Butler, United States Volunteer Service, while engaged in recruiting his Division, will command.

. . . .

By order.

L. THOMAS, *Adjutant-General.*

WAR DEPARTMENT, October 2, 1861.

Dear Sir,—You will arrange to pay the men now enlisted, and those to be mustered in the Eastern States, by General B. F. Butler, the amount of pay that would be due them for the first month's pay from the date they are mustered into the service of the United States. This payment, in advance, is strongly recommended by the General in command, and the requisition will be met by the Secretary of the Treasury.

Please detail a competent Paymaster for the command, and give him full instructions to enable him to comply promptly with this Order.

Very respectfully,

SIMON CAMERON, *Secretary of War.*

Col. LARNED, *Paymaster-General.*

[Telegram.]
WAR DEPARTMENT, WASHINGTON,
October 2, 1861.

To Governor ANDREW, *Boston*:

Send the three regiments for General Sherman to Hempstead Camp on Long Island by Monday morning at the latest. Earlier if possible.

SIMON CAMERON, *Secretary of War.*

[Telegram.]
WAR DEPARTMENT, WASHINGTON,
October 3, 1861.

To Governor ANDREW, *Boston:*

Send the Wilson Regiment to Washington direct. Give Sherman the next one as soon as possible.

SIMON CAMERON, *Secretary of War.*

HEAD-QUARTERS, DEPARTMENT OF NEW ENGLAND,
BOSTON, October 5, 1861.

To His Excellency JOHN A. ANDREW:

Sir,—I herewith enclose a copy of General Order No. 1, in which I assume command of the Department of New England.

I have the honor to be, very respectfully,
  Your Excellency's most obedient servant,
    BENJ. F. BUTLER, *Major-General commanding.*

HEAD-QUARTERS, DEPARTMENT OF NEW ENGLAND,
BOSTON, October 5, 1861.

[*General Order, No.* 1.]

By order of the President of the United States, the six New England States are constituted the Department of New England under the command of Major-General B. F. Butler, head-quarters at Boston.

The Major-General commanding announces his staff as follows:

Major George E. Strong, Assistant Adjutant-General, acting officer of ordnance and chief of staff.

Captain Peter Haggerty and Lieutenant W. H. Wiegel, Aides-de-Camp.

Gilman Kimball, Brigade Surgeon, Medical Director.

Captain Paul R. George, Brigade Quartermaster, Assistant-Quartermaster.

All officers in command of troops mustered in the service of the United States will report either in person or by letter to these head-quarters.

The quarterly and monthly returns of the several United States officers in this department for the 30th of September not already forwarded, will be forwarded to these head-quarters. The attention of such officers is called to the regulations which require such communications to be made to the chief of staff.

Full returns of the material in the Commissary, Quartermaster and Ordnance departments under the charge of United States officers are required forthwith.

By command of Major-General Butler.

Peter Haggerty,
A. D. C. and Acting Assistant Adjutant-General.

Head-Quarters, Department of New England,
Boston, October 5, 1861.

My Dear Sir,—Being desirous of raising some men in New England, for special purpose, to be armed and equipped with reference thereto, I asked the authorization of the President of the United States to raise them and he gave it to me, and telegraphed for your assent, as well as the governors of other New England States.

Your assent was given; acting upon that, I called upon you and you desired that I should wait a week, when the regiment of Colonel Wilson, then being recruited, would be full before I took any action upon that subject. To this I assented, and have been only looking out for my officers, for recruiting purposes, and have made no public announcement, and allowed one who had a special corps to make advertisement which I thought, would be fully within the spirit of the understanding.

I then shew you an Order to take regiments already raised and not assigned to other officers, for another purpose, and you offered to assign me Colonel Jones' Regiment. You also said that an Irish regiment now being raised, you would like to be assigned to me, to that I assented, and left for the purpose of oganizing recruiting in Maine and from thence to Washington. On my return I find that the recruiting officers have been making publications injurious to me and the recruiting service, so that it becomes necessary to know what exactly is understood between us.

Two weeks have passed and now these regiments are not full, the allegations of men are, that they will not serve under some of the officers which have been appointed. I desire therefore, the simple announcement by General Order, that I have authority to enlist men for a regiment, to be numbered as you please, also a squadron of mounted men. These troops to be a part of the Volunteer force of the State. These to be in addition to those already assigned by you. If you choose however to recall the Irish regiment assigned me, I shall have no objections. I should be glad to keep it, but I should be unjust to others if I did so, to the exclusion of a new regiment. That being done, I see no difficulty in the way of filling up all these regiments at once, save this one.

A most vicious practice has arisen here, as it seems to me, of captains or other recruiting officers offering private bounties for men, of five and seven dollars. This amounts in fact to the sale of men by the recruiting officers to the captain, who has the most money, to fill up his company. The men hold off from enlisting for a higher bid, and so the deserving, but poor officer gets no men to enlist, and the whole recruitment is demoralized. This bounty can only be got from the officers, and it amounts to the British system of buying commissions in its worst form. I will not tolerate it where I have the authority so to do, and I would respectfully suggest its evil tendency in others.

I trust these suggestions and this course which will allow those patriotic persons who have done me the honor to inform me of their desire to enlist in the service of the country, to serve under my command in preference to another, the opportunity of so enlisting while others of different preferences will have an opportunity to gratify their desires, and both classes will thus be brought at once into the field where they are so much needed. At your Excellency's request, I have put this matter in writing to prevent possible misunderstanding.

With sentiments of the highest respect,

I am most truly yours,

BENJ. F. BUTLER, *Major-General commanding*.

To His Excellency JOHN A. ANDREW, *Commander-in-Chief*.

[Copy of Major-General Butler's Enlistment papers.]

United States Volunteers Enlistment List.

We, the undersigned, by our signatures hereto, do hereby severally agree to serve for a period of three years from the date of our enlistment, in the United States service, or during the war, unless sooner discharged, as volunteers in the force called for by the President in his proclamation of May 3d, 1861, in accordance with the terms of said proclamation and under the organization set forth in General Orders from the war department and from the adjutant-general's office; and if ordered into camp and our number is not filled up to the minimum number of men, on or before the 20th day of October, we severally agree to serve in the companies to which we may be severally assigned.

Enlisted men are entitled to pay, subsistence, clothing and quarters from the term of their enlistment. Pay, $13 per month. A bounty of $100 upon being honorably discharged at the end of the war.

EXECUTIVE DEPARTMENT, BOSTON, $9\frac{1}{2}$, P. M., October 5, 1861.

Major-General BUTLER:

My Dear Sir,—I have just received and read your note of to-day's date, on my return from visiting our Cavalry Camp at Readville; and I beg leave to say at once, in reply to your remark relating to some supposed promise of mine, that I did not at any time say that while we were already raising so many regiments in Massachusetts I could consent to an embarrassment of the service by additional competition for recruits. But, while I assured you of my willingness, so far as it lay in my power, to assign to you, out of regiments in progress, our fair proportion, or more than that, of the six regiments you told me you wished to raise in New England, I have constantly declared that I could not concur in a policy which, by crowding the competition of regiments, would be fatal, or very dangerous to successful recruiting. And I apprehend that we have been already, of late, overdoing the business, by attempting to raise one cavalry and eight infantry regiments and three battery corps at the same time. I am convinced that four of these infantry regiments should first be filled, before beginning upon more regiments. The length of time we have already spent in recruiting these bodies now in process, to which fact your note alludes, is a circumstance confirmatory of this opinion. The 22d Regiment will march on Tuesday; the 23d, 25th and 27th will be filled, doubtless, by Monday week, if not disturbed by more competitors. And since all the regiments in New England are ordered to report to yourself, and there will be no difficulty in getting the troops needed for your own column, I need feel no anxiety in that respect. Please, however, send me a roster of company officers under whom you wish a new regiment enlisted, if you have any offering of whom you think favorably, and I will authorize a new regiment to begin in a week from Monday next, under Capt. Henry L. Abbott, (of Massachusetts,) of the U. S. Topographical Engineers, for Colonel, and Charles Everett, late Colonel of District Columbia Volunteers, formerly serving in Mexico, or Major Francis Brinley, for Lieutenant-Colonel—the Major to be selected seasonably.

I cannot authorize any earlier movement, especially in view of your proposal to advance half a month's pay to the new regiment, to the exclusion of the other regiments now recruiting; nor can I consent to the organization of *any regiment at any time* upon such a plan of favoritism. If gentlemen, out of their own purses, choose to offer bounties to secure enlistments, I know not that I can interpose to prevent it. But I do not approve of its being done, nor have I ever known an instance of the kind. If, however, any person employed in the general recruiting service, or any other agent of the Commonwealth, has ever in one instance taken money as a consideration for any thing done, or left undone, in relation to the duty or service touching which his employment gave him any power or function, I will be obliged to you, or to any other person, for the evidence of such fact. I should regard such conduct as a grave offence, which should not be suffered, and which should not be allowed to pass without full pursuit. And since you suggest that recruiting officers have sold men for a price to regimental or company commanders, I rely on your zeal for the public good, and your sense of what is due to justice, both to the public service and to individuals, that the guilty shall be specified and all the means of proof made known to me, in order that the most speedy and vigilant measures for suppression and rebuke may be instituted.

Since I began this note, permit me to add, that the first instance of the offering of private bounty has come to my knowledge, requiring me, therefore, to correct a statement made in the earlier part of this letter. And that is the case of a gentleman who had the offer from yourself of a commission in case he would enlist a given number of men, to secure which he has offered five dollars per man. I regret to be obliged to refer to this point, because I am grieved to know that any officer of the United States army has begun to interfere at all with enlistments for the Volunteer force in Massachusetts. Poor and humble as may be the value of my own services and judgment, and little as I may have personally contributed to the success of our military preparations and movements, yet I have the great satisfaction of knowing that we have pursued a *system*, carefully, watchfully, faithfully, and zealously, in which, by the intelligent and loyal co-operation of all officers of the State and of the Union, who have had any connection with such matters here, we have found reason to trust. In truth, almost any system is better than none. We have, thanks to the energy and zeal of the people of the Commonwealth, enlisted, armed, uniformed, equipped, and forwarded with complete camp material and baggage trains, sixteen full infantry regiments, to say nothing of two artillery corps and our sharpshooters; and the public, and the government, have observed their numbers, completeness and efficiency, with numberless expressions of approval and satisfaction. We are, at this very moment, doing half as much more, and doing it with the utmost of our ability, and we have, thus far, escaped the confusion and uncertainty of movement which have embarrassed some other States, and from which, by much effort, their Governors have only just now escaped. Now, with the utmost respect for the Department of War, and for yourself personally, and with the most loyal sentiment of obedience, I mean to continue to do just what I have from the first persistently done; and that is, to hold, with an iron hand and unswerving purpose, all the powers which, by the laws, pertain to me officially in my own grasp; yielding the most implicit obedience in all things to those having the right to direct me; but, at the same time, remembering that true subordination requires every officer to perform his own duties and fulfil his own functions himself, as well as to submit himself loyally to his official superiors. And I know that I have most earnestly and diligently, without stopping a moment to count the cost, endeavored to obey every requisition of the War Department, and to furnish every thing it desired. Now, the law and the army orders place the business of raising and recruiting for the volunteer service, and the commissioning of volunteer officers, in the hands of the Governors of the States from which they are called and by which they are furnished; nor is it permitted by law, to the President himself, even were he so disposed, to interfere in the premises, unless the Governor of a State on whom a call for troops is made refuses or neglects to perform his proper functions. And I am and have repeatedly been, assured, by the Secretary of War, that his Department regarded with the utmost satisfaction the efforts made by Massachusetts to serve the country and support the national arms; and, moreover, that he had issued no orders, and would issue none, tending to interfere with the State authorities.

I shall, therefore, do exactly by you as I have done by Gen. Sherman and Gen. Burnside; that is to say, I shall use every exertion to furnish troops for the service you propose, in our full proportion. But it must be done by pursuing such methods and plans as we have found necessary for the general advantage of the service. Nor can I permit, so far as it lies with me to decide, *any officers of the United States* to raise troops, as Massachusetts volunteers, within this Commonwealth, except for recruitment of existing regiments, or subject to the conditions indicated; while any advice or friendly assistance will be gratefully received from any quarter, much more from a gentleman of your capacity to advise, and your hearty zeal in the cause we are both aiming to serve.

'I have the honor to be, with high respect and regard,
Yours faithfully,
JOHN A. ANDREW.

[Statutes at Large, of the United States, passed at the First Session of the 37th Congress.]

CHAP. IX. An Act to authorize the Employment of Volunteers, &c.

Be it enacted, &c.:

SECT. 4. That * * * the Governors of the States furnishing volunteers under this act, shall commission the field, staff and company officers requisite for said volunteers; but in cases where the State authorities refuse or omit to furnish volunteers at the call, or on the proclamation of the President, and volunteers from such States offer their services under such call or proclamation, the President shall have power to accept such services and to commission the proper field, staff, and company officers.

[Telegram.]

EXECUTIVE DEPARTMENT, BOSTON,
October 5, 1861.

To Hon. SIMON CAMERON, *Secretary of War, Washington, D. C.:*

Will you pay our soldiers as fast as sworn in half month's pay, detailing paymaster therefor? Do not authorize this for any unless for all.

What is General Butler's power and position here?

JOHN A. ANDREW, *Governor.*

[Telegram.]

WAR DEPARTMENT, WASHINGTON, October 5.

To Gov. ANDREW, *Boston:*

We cannot pay in advance.

General Butler has authority to concentrate a brigade for special service, all of which is to be organized under the several Governors of the Eastern States.

We gave General Butler authority with regard to advance.

SIMON CAMERON, *Secretary of War.*

EXECUTIVE DEPARTMENT, BOSTON,
October 6, 1861.

Hon. SIMON CAMERON, *Secretary of War, Washington, D. C.*:

Sir,—I am very much at loss to attach a definite construction to your telegram, received last evening, in reply to my inquiry of you as to what is the power and the position of Major-General Butler in this Commonwealth, since the recent army orders assigning him to the command of a new military Department which includes the State of Massachusetts; and my perplexity on this subject is increased, by the official service upon me, at the same moment, of the annexed communication and Order from General Butler. I enclose to you the originals.

What am I to understand by this requirement, that all officers in command of troops mustered into United States service —without limitation as to time or place, shall report themselves to him?

On the 23d ultimo, I issued an Order respecting the volunteer regiments which are being raised in Massachusetts under my direction. I inclose to you a copy of this Order and invite your attention to it, and also to the General Order of the War Department of the United States, of the 16th ultimo, an extract from which is therein quoted.

You will perceive thereby that in Massachusetts I am engaged in recruiting at this time eight regiments of infantry from the 22d to the 29th inclusive, one regiment of cavalry, and three batteries of artillery—one battery having been completed and dispatched to Washington on Friday last. The 22d Infantry (Col. Wilson's) is under orders to leave for Washington to-morrow. Am I to understand that its departure must be delayed in order that its colonel shall report to General Butler? The 23d, 25th and 27th regiments are in an advanced state of preparation, and acting under authority from yourself, I have selected them to form the contingent desired from Massachusetts for General Sherman. Am I to understand now, that their colonels are to report to General Butler, and be liable to be diverted at his discretion, from the designation I have made concerning them? The 24th Regiment (Col. Stevenson) I have, under your authority, intended for General Burnside; am I to understand that this intention is subject to General Butler's permission?

When General Butler first came here with his plan for raising six regiments in New England, I at once assigned to him— subject to your approval—two (the 26th and 28th) of the eight regiments I then had started; nor is there any difficulty in his having a third, if need be. I regret his appearance now in the capacity of a recruiting officer, introducing as it does an element of confusion, perplexity, and conflict, into the system of raising and equipping troops which has thus far been steadily and earnestly pursued here.

Why is power given to him thus to interfere with me and distract and confuse the system under which my operations are conducted? I have not received from the President, nor from yourself any notice that my efforts to serve the country in my official capacity have not been efficient and satisfactory. On the contrary, the President and yourself have at various times given assurances—very gratifying in their terms—of a contrary description. If any thing has occurred to produce a revolution of opinion on this subject in your mind, I trust it may be disclosed; but in view of your recent expressions of satisfaction with what has been and is being accomplished in Massachusetts, the present attitude of General Butler puzzles me exceedingly.

I dread the introduction into Massachusetts of the same elements of confusion from which the executives of New York and Pennsylvania have just extricated themselves; and I desire to arrive at a thorough understanding at once with a view to harmonize matters before they become so entangled as to annihilate the military efficiency of this Commonwealth. This is my apology for writing to you thus earnestly and frankly.

To one circumstance I beg to call your especial attention. General Butler, it seems, comes clothed with some authority to pay half a month's advance to men enlisted by himself. How does it happen that *all* the troops raised here cannot receive advance pay, if it is proposed thus to favor *a part?* And why should this trust of discrimination be reposed in an officer who has been unfamiliar hitherto with the practical business of raising men in this State for the war? We have done our utmost to obey and to anticipate even the wishes of the Federal government in the enlistment of men and in the perfection and economy of their preparation and equipment, and I am more troubled by this disturbing interposition, than I have been by all the toils and responsibilities of the year.

I heartily desire to avoid collision or even the slightest complaint. I am willing to sacrifice any thing merely personal to myself, but I cannot consent in silence to the entering of a wedge for I know not what distractions to follow. Even now I begin to hear of persons who claim to have had commissions promised to them by General Butler, and if he undertakes to raise troops here himself he will undertake to control the appointment of their officers, although the Governor, alone, can by law grant commissions unless he shall refuse to exercise his functions and neglect to raise troops when required.

I beg leave, in conclusion, again to express to you my conviction of the necessity of immediate action by the President and yourself on the subjects I have thus presented, with a view clearly to understand the relation which it is intended to establish between General Butler's authority and my own, and to avoid the evils which must inevitably result from the present attitude of affairs.

I have the honor to be, very respectfully,
Your obedient servant,
JOHN A. ANDREW, *Governor of Massachusetts.*

EXECUTIVE DEPARTMENT, BOSTON,
October 7, 1861.

To Major-General B. F. BUTLER:

Sir,—His Excellency Governor Andrew directs me to say, that the pressure upon his time which has occupied him all of yesterday and to-day will continue this evening and through to-morrow, when he will be obliged to leave town for a day more; but that if you desire to communicate with him, and will do so in writing, directed to 71 Charles Street, this evening, he will endeavor to prepare a proper answer before morning, and cause it to be sent to you at an early hour.

Yours very truly,
THOMAS DREW, *Ass't Mil. Sec'y.*

RECRUITING OF TROOPS.

At Office, October 8, 1861, 10, A. M.

General Butler received his Excellency's note at this hour, which renders it almost impossible to prepare a written statement of the matter of communication.

A personal interview of five minutes would, in his judgment, conduce to the public service, and save explanation much more formal in writing.

If Governor Andrew has any reasons personal to General Butler for not desiring an interview (of which he is not aware) of course the interview is not desirable.

[The above has no signature nor address, but is in the handwriting of General Butler.]

Executive Department, October 8, 1861.

Major-General Butler,. *U. S. Volunteers:*

General,—His Excellency Governor Andrew has the honor to acknowledge the receipt of your letter of this morning, and directs me to reply that he has no reason whatsoever of a character personal to yourself for not desiring an interview; that, on the contrary, he has always had strong reasons to be pleased in your personal society, which has been invariably agreeable to him. But he is at this hour, and will continue to be for some time, engaged at a session of the Executive Council, and various other engagements of an imperative character are pressing upon his attention. Therefore, unless the subject upon which an interview is desired is of such a character as to absolutely require immediate attention, he would prefer at this moment that it should be placed in writing, especially in view of the fact that there appears by your letter of the 5th inst. to be a difference of memory respecting the oral conversation therein referred to.

I have the honor to be, your obedient servant,

A. G. BROWNE, Jr., *Lt.-Col. and Military Sec'y.*

HEAD-QUARTERS, NEW ENGLAND DEPARTMENT, }
BOSTON, October 8, 1861.

To His Excellency JOHN A. ANDREW, *Governor and Commander-in-Chief*:

Sir,—I desire to know if any rooms at the State House could be temporarily obtained, until the meeting of the Legislature, for the use of myself and staff as head-quarters.

Knowing that some rooms were put to the use of General Wilson, I am emboldened to make the request.

I have the honor to be, very respectfully,
Your obedient servant,
BENJ. F. BUTLER, *Major-General commanding*.

EXECUTIVE DEPARTMENT, October 8, 1861.

Major-General BUTLER:

Sir,—I have not the assignment of rooms in the State House. I found Col. Wilson occupying a room. It was not with my consent, but it was to the inconvenience of all having business in our wing of the building. I think it a bad precedent, and not to be followed; nor, so far as I may be consulted, can I consent that the State House shall be used as head-quarters or for office-rooms by any but those officers contemplated by law and having rooms regularly assigned to them, such as heads of departments and bureaus of the Commonwealth. I am informed to-day that Col. Wilson happened almost by accident to begin using the room he frequented; and knowing that his stay here would be very brief, and his hours few each day while here, I did not feel willing to ask his removal. And I am very sorry now, to be compelled by your reference to the fact of his presence here, to say a word about it.

I am, very respectfully yours,
JOHN A. ANDREW.

[Telegram.]
WAR DEPARTMENT, WASHINGTON, }
October 8, 1861.

To Governor ANDREW, *Boston*:

I have agreed that Wilson's Regiment should come to Washington, and you to furnish another regiment in its place.

SIMON CAMERON, *Sec'y of War*.

HEAD-QUARTERS, DEPARTMENT OF NEW ENGLAND,
BOSTON, October 12, 1861.

Will "His Excellency Governor Andrew," assign to General Butler the recruitment of a regiment of Massachusetts Volunteers, and a squadron of mounted men, to be armed and equipped by him under the authority of the President; the officers to be selected by General Butler but commissioned by "His Excellency," with, of course, a veto power upon what may be deemed an improper selection. As these officers are to go with General Butler upon duty, would "His Excellency" think it improper he should exercise the power of recommendation.

To the telegram of the President, asking consent that the authorization should be given to General Butler, to raise troops, "His Excellency" telegraphed in reply that he would "aid" General Butler to the utmost.

General Butler knows of no way in which "His Excellency" can aid him so effectually, as in the manner proposed.

The selection by "His Excellency," in advance, without consultation, of a colonel and lieutenant-colonel, of an unformed regiment, not a soldier of which has been recruited by the State, and both these gentlemen, to whom the General at present knows no personal objection, being absent from the State on other duty, seems to him very objectionable.

It is not certain that Lieut. Abbott, of the Topographical Engineers, will be permitted to leave his corps. Colonel Everett has not lived in the State for many years, and has not such interest identified with the State or the men of Massachusetts whom he would command, as to render his appointment desirable.

General Butler has had, and can have the aid of neither in his regiment, and he believes that those who do the work, other things being equal, should have the offices. General Butler would have been happy to have conferred with "His Excellency" upon these and other points, but "His Excellency" did not seem to desire it.

General Butler has proceeded upon this thesis in his recruitment,—to say to all patriotic young men, who seemed proper persons, and who have desired to enter the service as officers, "If you have the confidence of your neighbors, so that you can recruit a given number of men, then by giving evidence of your energy and capacity thus far, if you are found fit in other respects upon examination, I will recommend you for a commission, to command the number of men you shall raise.

This is believed to be a course much better calculated to find officers, than to hunt for them by the uncertain light of petitions and recommendations.

General Butler desires to make good his words to these young gentlemen. "His Excellency" will perceive the impossibility of at once furnishing a roster under such circumstances, as requested, for " His Excellency's " perusal.

"His Excellency's" attention is called to the fact, that no reply has been received to General Butler's request, as to a squadron of mounted men.

General Butler is informed, by the returns of those who have recruited for him, that he has already a number of men, equal to two regiments, in such progress that they can be organized in ten days, being the most prompt recruitment ever done in this State ; these besides the 26th and 28th Regiments, assigned to him by General Order.

General Butler trusts that " His Excellency " will not, without the utmost necessity for it, throw any obstacles in the way of his recruitment, as General Butler is most anxious to get his Division organized, so as to start upon an expedition already planned, in the service of his country.

General Butler hopes that these views will meet " His Excellency's " concurrence and co-operation.

Most respectfully, " His Excellency's " obedient servant,

BENJAMIN F. BUTLER.

EXECUTIVE DEPARTMENT, BOSTON, }
October 14th, 1861. }

To Major-General B. F. BUTLER, *U. S. Volunteers*, *commanding Department of New England*:

General,—I beg leave to acknowledge the receipt at this Department, of your letter of the 12th inst., addressed to His

Excellency Governor Andrew, which I have forwarded according to its direction, His Excellency being absent from the city.

I have the honor to be your obedient servant,

A. G. BROWNE, Jr., *Lt.-Col. and Military Secretary.*

Will A. G. Browne, Jr., give the bearer a descriptive Roll, and oblige yours,

P. HAGGARTY.

A. G. BROWNE, Jr., *Lieut.-Col. and Military Secretary,* State House.

[This bears no date, but was received by me on October 19th. A. G. BROWNE, Jr.]

CITY OF LOWELL, MAYOR'S OFFICE,
October 18, 1861.

To His Excellency Governor ANDREW:

Dear Sir,—There appears to be a question whether the men enlisting into General Butler's Division are entitled to State aid for their families. We have paid in several cases where it seemed to be absolutely necessary to do so. I have written the Adjutant-General upon this subject, and he sends me a printed copy of General Order No. 23, but I notice that was issued Sept. 23d, and it has occurred to me that perhaps this Order was not designed to cover the case to which I now call your Excellency's attention. I wish to act understandingly in paying money from the City Treasury. An early reply will therefore oblige

Your obedient servant,

B. C. SARGEANT, *Mayor.*

[*Endorsed.*—Executive Department, Boston, Oct. 21, 1861. Received this day and respectfully referred to the Attorney-General for answer.

By order of the Governor, A. G. BROWNE, Jr., *Lieut.-Col. and Military Secretary.*]

ATTORNEY-GENERAL'S OFFICE, October 23, 1861.

To His Honor B. C. SARGEANT, *Mayor of Lowell:*

Sir,—His Excellency Governor Andrew, has referred to me, for answer, your letter of the 18th, in which you inquire whether men enlisted in General Butler's Brigade are entitled to the benefits of the Act in aid of the families of volunteers.

In my opinion all volunteers who are inhabitants of this State and enlist in Massachusetts regiments should receive the benefits of this statute, and it includes all regiments raised in this State under the authority of the Governor, the officers of which are by him commissioned. If General Butler's Brigade is to be so raised and so commissioned, then its soldiers will be mustered into and enlisted in the service of the United States within the fair meaning of the language of the first section, " as members of the volunteer militia of the State." I suppose this will be the case, and therefore that the men enlisted by him will be entitled to the usual aid.

And I only state my opinion in this guarded form, because of the possible, but highly improbable contingency of volunteers being enlisted in full regiments in Massachusetts without the sanction of its Executive, the officers of which he might decline to commission or recognize.

Very respectfully your obedient servant,

DWIGHT FOSTER.

EXECUTIVE DEPARTMENT, October 23, 1861.

Hon. B. C. SARGEANT, *Mayor of Lowell:*

My dear Sir,—The Order No. 23 applies to all persons professing to recruit under whatever authority for any regiments other than those therein designated. I put at Major-General B. F. Butler's disposal the 26th Regiment and the 28th, and desired all the influence he could bring to bear upon recruiting should be made to avail for the benefit of these corps until they should be filled. They, as yet, are not full. I understand that persons—acting under his supposed authority, but wholly in defiance of my explicit statement to that gentleman of my own wish and purpose—assume to enlist men into other, or for other, organizations, not included in Order No. 23 ; thus introducing more competition, when we had already strained the recruiting as far as it was prudent, and thus putting back some ten infantry, cavalry, and artillery corps, in progress. If Genera Butler favors these persons, I am equally pained and surprised.

It is certainly without right and without authority, detrimental to the service and tending to some breach between himself and me, when we ought to work, each in our respective spheres, as the patient servants of a cause it is glory enough to serve in any manner, however humble. Had not this interference been attempted, some of our regiments would have been full, which are not yet quite complete ; when if another and third regiment was needed from Massachusetts to complete General Butler's six regiments of infantry he wished for, I would cheerfully before now have designated some officers to begin its recruitment.

The men whom General Butler or others in his interest have influenced to offer to enlist will be fully recognized as Massachusetts volunteers on going into any of Colonel Jones' companies (26th Regiment) or Colonel Murphy's (28th Regiment). And there is yet room for them.

I am, with high regard, your obedient servant,

JOHN A. ANDREW.

HEAD-QUARTERS, DEPARTMENT OF NEW ENGLAND,
BOSTON, October 21, 1861.

[*General Order, No. 2.*]

By the authority of the President of the United States, in words following :—

"WAR DEPARTMENT, Sept. 10, 1861.

"Major-General B. F. Butler is hereby authorized to raise, organize, arm, uniform and equip a Volunteer force for the war, in the New England States, not exceeding (6) six regiments of the maximum standard, of such arms, and in such proportions, and in such manner as he may judge expedient ; and for this purpose, his orders and requisitions on the Quartermaster, Ordnance, and other Staff Departments of the Army, are to be obeyed and answered ; provided the cost of such recruitment, armament, and equipment does not exceed, in the aggregate, that of like troops now or hereafter raised for the service of the United States.

"SIMON CAMERON, *Secretary of War.*

"Approved Sept. 12, 1861.

"A. LINCOLN."

And with the consent, by telegram to the War Department, of their Excellencies the Governors of the several States wherein the troops are proposed to be raised, the Commanding-General of the Department of New England proposes to recruit not exceeding six regiments of the maximum number of the various arms; and, for that purpose, has authorized recruitment in the several States of Massachusetts, Connecticut, Vermont, New Hampshire, and Maine.

In order to correct any mistake or misunderstanding, the officers recruiting are empowered to enlist men in the service of the United States upon the terms following, and no other:—

The troops are to be regiments or corps of the several States in which they are enlisted, and are to be deemed a part of the quota thereof. The officers to be commissioned by the Governors of the several States, according to the Constitution and Laws thereof, and of the United States. Pay to be thirteen dollars ($13) per month, and one hundred dollars ($100) bounty at the end of the war, to the honorably discharged soldier. All the troops of this Division to be paid at least one month's pay before they leave their respective States or the camp of instruction, so as to be able to leave that sum with their families.

In Massachusetts, towns and cities are empowered, by an Act of the legislature, to relieve the families and relatives, within a certain degree, of every inhabitant of the State who shall enlist in the service; and, in the other New England States, bounties are offered and provision made for the support of the families of the enlisted soldier, and the troops raised under this Order will be entitled to all the bounty and relief provided by law for the volunteers of the several States. Especially will this be the case in Massachusetts, were there doubts otherwise, since his Excellency Governor Andrew telegraphed to the War Department that he " would help General Butler to the utmost " in his recruiting.

A vicious practice having come to the notice of the Commanding-General of other sums being paid by officers recruiting in the State of Massachusetts, it is positively forbidden to any person recruiting under the authority of the United States, to offer, promise, or give any money or valuable thing whatever for recruits to any person; and any person so offending will not be recommended for commission by the Commanding-General.

No recruits are desired who are habitually intemperate, or who have ever been convicted of any crime. Deserters from the British army are especially reprobated. It is the wish and desire of the Commanding-General to have in his Division only thoughtful, patriotic men, who are seriously desirous of aiding their country in her hour of peril, and who will enlist under her banner for this reason alone.

All recruits will be immediately taken into camp upon their enlistment; will be uniformed in the best manner, instructed by competent drill masters in the appropriate exercises for their proper arm of service, and their health and comfort specially cared for. In return for this, the most thorough subordination, discipline, and good conduct will be exacted. As soon as the Division, thus raised, is brought into a proper state of efficiency, it will march, under the orders of the Commanding-General, upon a service already designated, and to which it is to be fitted.

The numbers and names of regiments and corps will be hereafter designated by General Order.

By command of Major-General Butler.

GEO. C. STRONG, *Assistant Adjutant-General.*

HEAD QUARTERS, DEPARTMENT OF NEW ENGLAND,
BOSTON, October 25, 1861.

To His Excellency Governor ANDREW:

Under authority given me of date of September 10th, by the War Department of the United States, a copy whereof has heretofore been sent to your Excellency, there has been enlisted and mustered into the service of the United States a company of Massachusetts volunteers, numbering eighty-six (86) men, inhabitants of said State. A copy of the descriptive list of said company is herewith forwarded for deposit in the office of the Adjutant-General of the State.

These men have severally taken the oath required by law for enlisted men in the service of the United States, and are now in course of instruction at "Camp Chase," Lowell.

At Camp Chase, all the members of this company being present, (saving those absent without leave,) by written ballots, in my presence, the members of the company of twenty-one (21) years and upwards, selected their officers by election, as follows:

For Captain, Cadwallader F. Blanchard, of Lowell, who received eighty-three votes; all others, (E. A. Fiske,) one vote.

For 1st Lieutenant, James Parsons, of Lowell, who received fifty-nine votes; all others, (E. A. Fiske,) twenty-three votes.

For 2d Lieutenant, Edward A. Fiske, of Lowell, who received seventy-nine votes, (all others, eligible,) Ira Moore, one vote.

These gentlemen being thus severally elected in accordance with the principles of the Constitution, of Massachusetts, chapter 2, section 10, severally signified their acceptance of the trust reposed in them, and are approved and recommended by me, as persons fit to be appointed and commissioned in their respective offices.

If expedient, after they are commissioned, they may be reported for examination by a board appointed under the law for that purpose by the General commanding the department.

The President, in accordance with the Act of Congress, approved July 22, 1861, by authority vested in the General commanding this department, has accepted the service of this company of volunteers. They have been mustered into the service of the United States, in accordance with General Orders from the Adjutant-General's office, No. 58 and No. 1 of the current series.

Said Blanchard, Parsons and Fiske, have been duly mustered into the service, and have been duly selected by the written votes of the members of said company, for their several offices, in accordance with the principles of the Constitution of Massachusetts.

It therefore becomes my duty most respectfully to request your Excellency to commission these, the requisite company officers, so selected and recommended, in compliance with the requisitions of said Act of Congress, section 5, which provides that the Governors of States furnishing volunteers under this Act, shall commission the field, staff, and company officers requisite for the said volunteers to their offices.

If your Excellency knows or is informed of any personal disqualification in either of said officers, I respectfully ask that such disqualification may be stated, that others may be selected to be commissioned by the Governor of the State.

I have the honor to be, most respectfully,

Your obedient servant,

BENJAMIN F. BUTLER,
Commanding Department of New England, and authorized to raise troops as before stated.

EXECUTIVE DEPARTMENT, October 26, 1861.

To Major-General B. F. BUTLER, *U. S. Volunteers, Commanding Department of New England:*

General,—I beg leave to acknowledge your letter, dated the 25th inst., but not delivered by your messenger until this evening, and not accompanied by the descriptive list therein mentioned.

I respectfully decline to issue commissions to the gentlemen for whom you therein request them, and if the descriptive list of the men over whom you desire that officers shall be placed had been forwarded by you, I should have directed the Adjutant-General not to deposit it in his office. This refusal is altogether independent of the military qualifications of the gentlemen for whom you request commissions, and is caused entirely by the fact that these men who are assumed by you to have been properly organized into a company of Massachusetts Volunteers, have in reality been collected without due authority, in violation of law and of the express terms of an Order of the War Department of the United States, of a date subsequent to that of the authorization you rely upon in your General Order, No. 2, of the Department of New England, and also in violation of a General Order, (No. 23,) issued at my direction by the Adjutant-General of this Commonwealth, as well as to the detriment of the several volunteer regiments now encamped in this Commonwealth, not yet recruited to the maximum standard.

By authority from the War Department, under date of September 10, you are authorized to raise six (6) regiments in New England.

By a General Order of the same Department, under date of September 16, "*all persons* having received authority from the

War Department to raise volunteer regiments, batteries or companies in the loyal States, *are, with their commands hereby placed under the order of the Governors of those States*, to whom they will immediately report the present conditions of their respective organizations. These troops will be organized or re-organized and prepared for service *by the Governors* of the respective States, *in the manner they* judge most advantageous for the interests of the general government."

And the special application of this Order to yourself is confirmed by a telegraphic despatch from the Secretary of War to myself, which states that " *General Butler has authority to concentrate a brigade for special service, all of which is to be organized under the several Governors of the Eastern States ;*" and also, by the reply of the Secretary of War to a letter from myself, making inquiry concerning the orders and authority under which you are assuming to act, in reference to which the Secretary of War wrote :

" It was the intention of this department to leave to your Excellency all questions concerning the organization of troops in your State, and the orders to which you refer were designed to be subject to the direction and control of the Executive of Massachusetts."

Conformably therewith, by my command, General Order No. 23 was issued by the Adjutant-General of Massachusetts, of which I inclose a copy, prohibiting the formation of any new regiment or companies in this State, without orders from these head-quarters, for the reason that it was of the first importance that the eight regiments of infantry, one of cavalry, and four batteries of artillery, which were then in process of organization in Massachusetts, should be completed without the delay which would be caused by additional competition.

I assigned to you the 26th Regiment, (Colonel Jones,) and the 28th Regiment, (Colonel Thomas S. Murphy,) as the fair proportion which Massachusetts should contribute to the brigade of six regiments which you desired to obtain from New England ; and being desirous to help you to the utmost, I even offered, so soon as such a time should elapse as would probably be sufficient to complete the recruiting of some of the nine regiments then in progress, to begin to organize a third regiment for you, (being more than the proportion of Massachusetts of the six,) and to offer its command to an experienced officer of the Topographical Engineers, who I had previously ascertained would have been willing to accept it.

You declined this additional offer, and it is against my orders that you have proceeded to collect men, and undertake to organize them under military form. By this action you have retarded and confused the recruiting service throughout the Commonwealth, have deprived several Massachusetts regiments of participation in important military operations now in progress, and to which they had been pre-assigned, by diverting recruits who might otherwise have filled their ranks, under promises of peculiar privilege as to pay; and, more than all, you have set an example of insubordination, especially lamentable in the instance of an officer of so high rank.

If the eighty-six men mentioned by you in your letter, desire to enter the service as Massachusetts Volunteers, I will order them to be drafted into the Twenty-Sixth (26th) Regiment, if there is yet room for them there, or into the Twenty-Eighth (28th) Regiment, which is only partially recruited, (and to which, though assigned to you, I do not learn that you have given any attention.) If they desire to serve their country efficiently, they will find opportunity there. Or, (though I do not desire to withdraw them from regiments destined for your command,) if neither of those corps are satisfactory, they can be furnished with service in other Massachusetts regiments.

I desire to call your attention, General, to the fact that the General Order, No. 2, issued by yourself as Commander of the Department of New England, does not properly represent the relation which the men collected by you against my orders hold to the executive authorities and the legislative acts of this Commonwealth, and unless modified, is likely to cause much individual perplexity and distress. In the same Order you have quoted a single sentence from a telegraphic despatch sent by me to the President of the United States, in such a manner and in such an association with other words, as to give a mistaken impression of its meaning, and of my own purposes and position.

I cannot conclude this note without an expression of keen regret that my plain and clearly defined official duty has brought me into any collision with a gentleman, whom in other spheres I have known so long, whose capacity and zeal for the public service is unquestioned by me, and between whom and myself there ought to be nothing inconsistent with cordial, patriotic and friendly co-operation in the support and defence of a cause grand as the proportions of the heritage of our fathers, and blessed as their own immortality of fame.

I am respectfully and obediently yours, &c., &c.,

JOHN A. ANDREW,
Governor and Commander-in-Chief of the Commonwealth of Massachusetts.

HEAD-QUARTERS, DEPARTMENT OF NEW ENGLAND, }
BOSTON, Nov. 6, 1861. }

To His Excellency Governor ANDREW:—

I beg leave to call His Excellency's attention to the fact that I have received no answer to my note of October 12, the receipt of which was acknowledged by His Excellency's Secretary in his absence.

In the fear that it may not have reached His Excellency, I have ventured to call attention to it, and also to know if any reply may be expected.

Very respectfully, your obedient servant,

BENJ. F. BUTLER, *Major-General commanding.*

EXECUTIVE DEPARTMENT, BOSTON, }
November 6, 1861. }

Major-General BENJ. F. BUTLER :

SIR,—I have the honor to reply, that on no consideration will the enlistment or organization of any cavalry or dragoons or mounted soldiers be permitted in this Commonwealth for the volunteer service until the First Cavalry Volunteer Regiment under Colonel Robert Williams shall have been fully organized and ready to march.

I have the honor to be,
Your ob't serv't,

JOHN A. ANDREW.

HEAD-QUARTERS, SPRINGFIELD, Nov. 11, 1861.

Adjutant-General WILLIAM SCHOULER, *State House, Boston:*

General,—It having been represented to the Governor a few days since, by Colonel Thomas G. Stevenson, commanding 24th Massachusetts Volunteers, that Major-General Butler had sent him an order to deliver up some five men, mustered into the United States service in the 24th Regiment, the Governor directed Colonel Stevenson not to deliver up the men.

His Excellency now learns that General Butler sent an order to Colonel Dimmick, commanding at Fort Warren, this morning, to have these same men delivered up to him, and this order could not be executed, as the names of the men were not given. At the same time Colonel Dimmick intimated to Colonel Stevenson, that if the names of any of the men were given by General Butler, he would feel bound to deliver them on the order.

The Governor directs me to state, that General Butler has no authority to enlist men in Massachusetts, unless for the regular army, excepting such as he shall enlist in those regiments which he is authorized to raise by the Governor,—to wit, the 26th and 28th Regiments. If, therefore, the men claimed by General Butler, were not enlisted either in the 26th or 28th, His Excellency orders that Colonel Stevenson shall not give them up, General Butler having no claim upon them; and if Colonel Stevenson cannot protect these men at Fort Warren, he is ordered to remove them to his camp at Readville.

You will issue orders to this effect to Colonel Stevenson without delay and with the utmost despatch.

I have the honor to be, very respectfully,
Your ob't serv't,
HARRISON RITCHIE, *Lieut.-Col. Aide-de-Camp.*

HEAD-QUARTERS, BOSTON, Nov. 12, 1861.
[*Special Order, No. 570.*]

It having been represented at these Head-Quarters that Major-General Butler, in command of the Department of New England, sent to Colonel Stevenson, 24th Regiment Massachusetts Volunteers, an order to deliver up to him certain soldiers in said

24th Regiment mustered into the United States service, which order Colonel Stevenson did not obey;—the Commander-in-Chief approves Colonel Stevenson's conduct.

Major-General Butler has no authority to enlist men in Massachusetts, (unless for the regular army,) excepting for those regiments which he was authorized to raise by his Excellency the Commander-in-Chief, viz.: the 26th and 28th. If, therefore, the men claimed by General Butler were not enlisted in either the 26th or 28th Regiment, Colonel Stevenson shall not give them up. If Colonel Stevenson cannot protect and hold his men at Fort Warren, he shall immediately remove them to camp Massasoit, Readville, and hold them until otherwise ordered.

Colonel Stevenson is charged with the execution of this Order.

By order of His Excellency JOHN A. ANDREW, *Governor and Commander-in-Chief.*

WILLIAM SCHOULER, *Adjutant-General.*

EXECUTIVE DEPARTMENT, BOSTON, November 27, 1861.

Brigadier-General THOMAS, *Adjutant-General U. S. Army:*

General,—For the sake of nearly a thousand misled men, who now occupy a position most unfortunate for themselves and their families, I beg to request your attention to the following considerations, concerning the troops which Major-General Butler has raised, contrary to my orders, and without authority from any source entitled to confer it.

Referring to my letters, addressed to that officer, under date of October 5th and October 26th, last, copies of which have been filed in the War Department, I would recall to your recollection, that by General Order No. 78, issued by you, on September 16th, General Butler was placed under my orders, in respect to recruiting in Massachusetts any portion of the force which, by authority from the War Department, dated September 10th, he was empowered to raise in New England, and also, that under date of September 27th, I was assured by the Secretary of War as follows:—

"It was the intention of this Department to leave to your Excellency all questions concerning the organization of troops in your State, and the Orders to which you refer, [i. e. those concerning General Butler,] were designed to be subject to the approval and control of the Executive of Massachusetts."

Also, that under date of October 5th, the Secretary telegraphed as follows, in reply to an inquiry from me, as to General Butler's power and position here :—

"General Butler has authority to concentrate a brigade for special service, all of which is to be organized under the several Governors of the Eastern States."

By reference to my letters of Oct. 5th, and Oct. 26th, before mentioned, and to facts well known to you from other sources, you are aware that in disobedience to my orders, General Butler proceeded to recruit an irregular force in Massachusetts, which now amounts to nearly a thousand men, and it is of those I wish to speak.

The fair proportion of Massachusetts in the six regiments General Butler was expected to obtain from New England, was two regiments. Accordingly I assigned to him our 26th and 28th, the first in an advanced state of preparation, and the latter in a condition most favorable to speedy recruitment and organization. Desiring to perfect his force in every arm of the service, so far as was consistently in my power, I also commenced to recruit for him the 4th Massachusetts Light Artillery Battery.

At that time, there were recruiting in the State eight regiments of infantry, one of cavalry, and four artillery batteries. Notwithstanding the fact that I might thereby create too great a strain on our capacity to raise men, in my desire to aid him, I, on October 5th, offered to commence after a short interval, the recruitment for his expedition of a third regiment, (being much more than the Massachusetts proportion of his six,) but this offer he declined ; and against my orders, and conflicting with the regular recruiting system of the State, and retarding the completion of all the regiments then in progress for Generals Sherman and Burnside, he proceeded to assemble the irregular force I have described, which is scattered throughout the Commonwealth, in various camps from Lowell to Pittsfield.

CORRESPONDENCE.

You are aware that I have declined to commission the officers over the force thus irregularly raised, or to organize it into regiments; and you have approved of my determination in that respect. But the services of these men ought not to be lost to the country, and however much they may be charged with responsibility for the insubordinate means by which they were collected, yet I trust that they may be disposed of in such a manner as to enable them to be properly officered, and to admit their families to the benefits (now denied to them) provided by chapter 222 of the Massachusetts statutes of 1861, known as the "Soldiers' Families' Relief Act." This chapter of our statutes, which became a law on May 23d last, instituted a system of public charity towards the needy families of our troops, varying in amount from $1 per week to $12 per month, according to the necessities of each case.

In dispensing this charity, (for further details of which please refer to the copy of the Act herewith inclosed,) the municipal authorities of our towns and cities act as the agents of the Commonwealth, and look to the descriptive rolls of our troops, on deposit in the office of our Adjutant-General, as *prima facie* evidence of entry in United States service, of the soldiers whose families apply to them for relief. But the descriptive rolls of General Butler's irregular troops are not received at that office, such troops not being raised under any authority from the Commonwealth; and our Attorney-General has rendered an official opinion concerning the "Relief Act," to the effect that its provisions apply only to such troops as are raised in this State, "under the authority of the Governor, and the officers of which are by him commissioned." You will perceive then in what an unfortunate condition in reference to this charity, these men are therefore placed.

In consideration of all these facts, I think that orders should be issued from the War Department at once regulating this matter. The men have been sworn into the United States service by officers under General Butler's direction; and they can be used to good advantage in recruiting up the 28th Regiment, (now about 750 strong,) which would have been filled to the maximum number some weeks since had it not been harrassed by this irregular and insubordinate competition. The surplus, after filling the 28th, cannot be better employed than in recruiting our 15th and 20th Regiments, which suffered at Ball's Bluff, and in completing the companies which I am authorized to raise to constitute an additional Massachusetts regiment, in combination with the seven companies which now constitute the Massachusetts Battalion at Fortress Monroe and Newport News.

I feel that I have presented ample reasons for *immediate* action by the War Department in regard to these men, in the facts :—

1. That they are now commanded by no legally constituted officers, and therefore not subject to proper military command.

2. That by disposing of them in the manner I propose, no less than four regiments, *i. e.* the 28th, 15th, 20th, and that at Fortress Monroe, all of them now defective or crippled, would be put in condition for immediately effective service.

3. That by such a disposition, their families, many of which are in great need, would become entitled to the benefits of the State relief act.

4. That a fruitful cause of discontent, strife, and embarrassment would be effectually removed.

I beg to call your attention further, in this connection, to the fact, that by Major-General Butler's order, the 4th Massachusetts Light Artillery Battery, which I raised for his expedition, was last week, without my knowledge, placed on board the steamer Constitution and despatched to sea ; none of its officers having been commissioned, and no application having been made to me, from any source, to appoint or commission them ; and no notice having been given to me of any intention to remove the battery, at that time, or in that manner, from the State. If proper notice had been given to me from any source, of General Butler's desire that the battery should sail at that time, I should have been happy to have completed its organization by the appointment of officers. But the first notice I received concerning the matter, was a hasty letter from one of the members of the battery, addressed to the Adjutant-General of the State, dated "On board Steamer Constitution, Boston Harbor, Nov. 21, 1861," and stating that it was at sea by Gen. Butler's command, and was under the direction of men purporting to be officers, who had been elected by the remaining men at a caucus convened by General Butler's order.

With regard to some of these men, presuming thus to act as officers, charges are on file in this Department, which, if substantiated, prove them to be persons of infamous character, unfit for any station of personal trust, honor, or responsibility.

The 26th Regiment, which sailed in the Constitution, and is one of the regiments raised by me and assigned to General Butler, was fully recruited, carefully uniformed and equipped by the State, and its officers were duly appointed and commissioned by me. But this battery was hurried away, without my knowledge, unofficered, incompletely uniformed and equipped, not fully recruited, not having any of its rolls prepared or deposited in the Adjutant-General's office, and utterly unfit for service.

In making these suggestions and representations to you, General, I am oppressed by an inexpressible feeling of regret, and almost of humiliation, that in this time of trouble I should be found, even under compulsion, complaining of any person or of any grievance. And if I had no public function, nor any duty other than to myself, I would be silent. But the public service requires obedience, subordination, decorum and respect to constituted authority, from all, to insure good order and the rights of all. And since Major-General Butler returned to New England in September last, authorized to concentrate a force here "*subject*" so far as concerned this Commonwealth "*to the approval and control of the Executive of Massachusetts, all of which force was to be organized under the several Governors of the Eastern States,*" and in view of the facts:—

1. That the policy of the War Department was clearly avowed to be non-interference with our enlistments.

2. That I assigned to General Butler our full quota, and a battery besides, of the force he was authorized to secure.

3. That in my letter to the Secretary of War, under date of October 6th, (to which I beg to refer you, and to which no reply or acknowledgment has ever been received by me,) I avowed clear and commanding reasons, why our recruitment should not be further crowded by competition, to which reasons they being also presented to General Butler in my letter to him of October 5th, he never has ventured any reply or objection.

4. That notwithstanding, and without my consent and against my declared will, and contrary to my General Order

No. 23, (a copy of which you will find annexed to my letter of October 6th to the Secretary,) issued conformably to the General Order of the War Department No. 78, and in defiance of my rightful "*control*," General Butler assumed to raise other and irregular bodies of soldiers, paying no heed, and bestowing no care to the 28th Regiment, which was placed at his disposal.

5. And that General Butler has long ago been informed by me, in writing, that I had determined not to organize such bodies of irregular troops, or grant commissions to officers over them;—from which determination I feel it to be my public duty not to depart:—

I feel that I cannot in justice to these men whom he has thus deluded into his movement, leave them sworn into United States service, as I understand them to have been, without at least this effort to secure to them a position in the service where they will be recognized by this Commonwealth as its regular troops, and whereby their families may become entitled to the benefits of the aid provided by law for the needy families of soldiers raised under the sanction of the authorities of Massachusetts.

And here I deem it my duty deliberately and earnestly to request that the appointment of Major-General Butler to the command of the Department of New England shall be revoked, or that the Commonwealth of Massachusetts, at least, shall be annexed to the Department of New York or to any other Department found most convenient.

No want was felt by us of any change from our connection with the old "Department of the East," nor was such change asked for or desired by any one to be affected by it, so far as I can learn, save by the Commander of the New Department of New England himself.

I make this request as well from self-respect as from conviction of its rightfulness; and I urge it with all the earnestness which can become me in a matter of the utmost concern—because in view of the utterly contemptuous manner in which Major-General Butler has conducted in the matter to which allusion has been made above, and the system of studious insult which he has practiced towards this Commonwealth, and the lawful powers which it is my duty to uphold, I cannot quietly endure longer without remonstrance. If I should continue silent, I should become an accomplice. I should help to discourage other good men who depend on my own manhood and fidelity, and official as well as personal honor, to maintain my proper authority, and make good my warranties expressed or implied in the orders and authorities issued and imparted by me relative to the subject of raising troops in this State for the Federal Volunteer service.

Moreover, the departure of Major-General Butler for another and remote theatre of action, to which he announces that he is bound, will leave the Department without any commander within reach of the duties, *if any*, which pertain properly to its command.

I had hoped that my letter of October 6th, to the Honorable Secretary of War, would have resulted in some authoritative regulation of all these matters, without obliging me further to assume the apparent attitude of accusation or of controversy. But the assumption of General Butler, as I learn from the public prints and from public report, to organize a regiment, and his persistency in demeaning himself in a manner which leaves me no assurance that my own efforts to raise the new regiments for which requisition has been made upon me by the Department, may not be interfered with or even defeated by other and more extensive usurpations on his part, oblige me to take a stand where we now are, to ask for a proper disposition of existing facts and for immunity for the future.

I address this letter to you, General, in order that it may be laid before the President, or the Secretary of War, or the General-in-Chief, by yourself, as the head of the appropriate bureau of communication, according to your judgment of the necessity and propriety of the case; and I have the honor to remain,

Most respectfully, your obedient servant,

JOHN A. ANDREW, *Governor of Massachusetts.*

HEAD-QUARTERS OF THE ARMY, ADJUTANT-GENERAL'S OFFICE,
WASHINGTON, December 3, 1861.

[*General Order, No. 105.*]

The following orders have been received from the Secretary of War:

I. No more regiments, batteries, or independent companies will be raised by the Governors of the States except upon the special requisition of the War Department.

Those now forming in the various States will be completed under direction of the respective Governors thereof, unless it be deemed more advantageous to the service to assign the men already raised to regiments, batteries or independent companies now in the field in order to fill up their organizations to the maximum standard prescribed by law.

By command of Major-General McClellan.

L. THOMAS, *Adjutant-General.*

HEAD-QUARTERS, DEPARTMENT OF NEW ENGLAND,
BOSTON, December 17, 1861.

To His Excellency JOHN A. ANDREW, *Governor and Commander-in-Chief:*

Governor,—On the 27th day of November there was forwarded to the Adjutant-General of the Commonwealth a letter of which the enclosed is a copy. No answer has been returned to that letter, and no action taken on its request. May General Butler request His Excellency to favor him with a reply, whether he will or will not commission the officers therein named. If any are objectionable General Butler would be pleased to be informed of the objections and will recommend others. As this Battery was raised under the authority of the State, and with His Excellency's approval, it did not seem to come within either the spirit or the letter of His Excellency's refusal to commission any officers for troops raised under the authority of the War Department for General Butler. A reply to this communication either in refusal or acquiescence would be but justice to the acting officers of this Battery but a matter of entire indifference to

His Excellency's ob't serv't,

BENJ. F. BUTLER, *Major-General commanding.*

HEAD-QUARTERS, DEPARTMENT OF NEW ENGLAND,
Boston, November 27, 1861.

General WILLIAM SCHOULER, *Adjutant-General State of Massachusetts:*

General,—I have the honor to enclose a list of the officers of the company known as the Salem Light Artillery, with a request that they may be commissioned by His Excellency the Governor, should they be deemed competent.

Captain Manning is understood to have been recommended by the Adjutant-General of the State.

Captain, Charles H. Manning; Lieutenants, Fred. W. Reinhardt, Joseph R. Salla, Henry Davidson, George W. Taylor. These officers have been duly elected by the said company.

By order of Major-General B. F. Butler.

I have the honor to be,
Very respectfully, your ob't serv't,
GEO. C. STRONG, *Assistant Adj't-Gen.*

EXECUTIVE DEPARTMENT, BOSTON,
December 17, 1861.

To Major General BUTLER:

General,—I am directed by His Excellency the Governor to state in reply to your note of this day, that it was his intention at the proper time to appoint and commission suitable officers for the 4th Battery, but that he was not advised of their intended removal from the Commonwealth, nor was any request made for such appointments, either from the company or from the acting officers, or from any other source, until eight days after the whole company had been removed from Massachusetts, when the Governor was requested by Major Strong to commission certain persons as officers, on the ground that they had been elected by the company, as it was said. But the company was gone. None of its rolls having been deposited in the office of the Adjutant-General, there were no means of identifying its men. At the time of Major Strong's request it was beyond the reach of any communication, nor was it easy to verify the qualifications of the persons suggested for officers except in so far as they were within the general knowledge of persons at the State

House. As to the person named for First Lieutenant, the information received by the Governor is that his character is such as to render him unfit for appointment. As to the one proposed for Fourth Lieutenant, he is said to have remained at home dangerously sick, nor has the Governor any information to justify the belief that he is physically fitted for service, or likely within a reasonable time to become so.

The Governor, with these exceptions, is not conscious of having any objections to the other appointments suggested in that company, if the opinions of those competent to judge confirm the alleged choice of the men, save that in his own judgment Mr. Sala is more competent to the captaincy than Mr. Manning. Being personally responsible to the company, to the people of the State and the country and to the cause of us all, for the appointments he makes, he is unwilling to permit those who are to be commanded to suffer the infliction of poor officers, even though suggested by themselves; and he has had frequent occasion during the year to relieve men from officers whom they had recommended or chosen and whose incompetency or unfitness was found by them to be intolerable. Nor is this strange, for the volunteers, unlike our militia, are not enlisted under circumstances, whether as to mutual acquaintance or intimate knowledge of proposed officers, or the means of ascertaining and comparing the respective merits of accessible candidates, favorable to the safe and successful selection of their officers, without much aid and protection against the practices of the designing and the ambitious.

The Governor is desirous of commissioning officers for the Battery, and would be glad to receive the testimonials, if any, on which the claims of the persons in this instance proposed for appointment, are founded.

I am directed, in conclusion, to suggest to you that the neglect to deposit in the office of the Adjutant-General proper descriptive rolls of the Battery, is liable to cause much inconvenience and distress to the families of its members, unless promptly remedied, for in administering the provisions of chapter 222 of the statutes enacted at the extra session of the legislature of this Commonwealth in May last, it is the habit of the municipal authorities of the towns and cities to look to such rolls for *prima facie* evidence of the entry into service of those soldiers whose families apply to them for relief, and also the habit of the State Auditor to make the same reference in auditing the municipal accounts of expenditures under the Act.

I have the honor to be your ob't serv't,

A. G. BROWNE, Jr.,
Lieut.-Col. and Military Secretary.

HEAD-QUARTERS, DEPARTMENT OF NEW ENGLAND, }
BOSTON, December 18, 1861. }

Lieut.-Col. A. G. BROWNE, Jr.,
Military Sec'y to His Excellency the Governor of Mass.:

Sir,—Major-General Butler, commanding the Department of New England, directs that the enclosed communication be respectfully returned to His Excellency Governor Andrew, as being of improper address and signature.

I am Col., very respectfully,
Your obedient servant,
GEO. C. STRONG, *A. A. General.*

BOSTON, December 18, 1861.

To Major-General BENJ. F. BUTLER, &c., &c., &c.

Sir,—Accustomed myself to attempt to reach the substance of duty through the forms of natural courtesy and propriety, which I do not willingly or wittingly offend, I make no doubt that my education and natural acuteness may both fail sometimes to instruct me in those technicalities of breeding which regulate the formal intercourse of society.

I beg you therefore not to hold *me* to such rigidness of propriety as by the letter of Major Strong, A. A. General, written this day to my Military Secretary, by your command, you have exacted of him.

Having myself seen and known the contents of the letter of Col. Browne, which is returned to him this day, with the criticism that it is not admissible, " as being of improper address and signature," I find myself unable to instruct him how to amend it, since the particulars of the offence were not stated, and were not discernable to me, nor, as I am assured, by him. I beg to assume all blame, if any there is, and to receive the proper correction as due to my own want of knowledge.

I have therefore ventured, as one citizen writing to another, in which capacity I may be less likely to offend propriety and unknown laws and usages, to beg leave to address myself to you; and, inclosing the objectionable letter, with Major Strong's reply, to ask the favor of a precise statement of the offence committed, and to be instructed what amendment would relieve it from all animadversion on its form both of address and signature.

And I have the honor to be,
Your most obedient servant,
JOHN A. ANDREW.

HEAD-QUARTERS, DEPARTMENT OF NEW ENGLAND,
BOSTON, December 19, 1861.

To His Excellency JOHN A. ANDREW,
Governor of Massachusetts:—

Sir,—I am instructed by Major-General Butler, to state, in reply to your Excellency's communication of yesterday, that the letter addressed by Lieut.-Col. Browne to General Butler, was returned, because in official correspondence, on military subjects, and between military men, it is customary to conform, if not to the letter of military law, (paragraph 449, last clause, Army Regulations,) at least to certain conventionalities equivalent thereto.

The letter to which that was a reply was addressed to *your Excellency*, and therefore signed by General Butler himself as claiming to be your Excellency's co-ordinate.

Lieut.-Col. Browne's letter was addressed not to the Chief of Staff at these head-quarters, but directly to the Major-General commanding the Department, and even then not in his official capacity.

General Butler desires me to state, moreover, that the proprieties above discussed are herein violated only because your Excellency's letter was received at the moment of General

CORRESPONDENCE. 57

Butler's departure for Washington, and he was therefore unable himself to respond, as was his desire to do.

I have the honor to be, Sir,
    Your Excellency's most obedient servant,
        GEORGE C. STRONG,
        A. A. General and Chief of Staff.

EXECUTIVE DEPARTMENT, BOSTON, }
December 20, 1861. }

To Major GEORGE C. STRONG, *Ass't Adj't General and Chief of Staff of Major-General Butler:*

Major:—I am directed by His Excellency Governor Andrew, to acknowledge the receipt this evening, of your letter bearing date yesterday, and to suggest to you certain misconceptions upon which it is written.

1. With the single exception of the President of the United States, no officer or person, whether State or National, civil or military, whether temporarily sojourning or permanently residing within the limits of Massachusetts, can be recognized, within such limits, as the "co-ordinate" of the Governor of the Commonwealth in official dignity or rank.

You are reminded of this fact simply because His Excellency would not seem to waive a point important in our federative system; of which system the President is the sole head, without any co-ordinate, and in which the States composing it are as essential to its constitutional life as are the people themselves, each respective Governor being the official head of his own State without any co-ordinate within his jurisdiction, saving the President of the United States, who is the Federal head, and the official superior of all magistrates and officers.

2. But irrespective of this fact, it appears very remarkable that a gentleman of acute perception and trained professional intellect, such as Major-General Butler has acquired by extensive experience in civil life, should quote the regulations for the army of the United States, as dictating ceremonies of official intercourse to a magistrate who is no part of that army, and not subject to its regulations, for it cannot admit of question that no regulations promulgated by the Secretary of War, and

liable to constant variation, can be imperative upon the Governor of a State, who, if General Butler's assertions of law and courtesy in this respect, are true, might, for the offence which General Butler alleges, be amenable to a court martial, and as a result of its finding be "dismissed from the service," which could only mean, be deposed from his office as Governor by the sentence of a court martial of the Federal army, if the theory be correct that his office is necessarily responsible to such army regulations.

But it needs no *reductio ad absurdum* to test the pretension that the Federal army regulations govern the Governors of the States, for in those regulations the catalogue of officers which they contemplate, is explicitly set forth, being from 1st to 16th (i. e. from lieutenant-general to corporal,) inclusive, and the Governors of the States are nowhere included in the enumeration ; nor does it seem to require argument to establish the fact that this *lex scripta* which is quoted by you under Major-General Butler's direction, to justify his abrupt and ungentle treatment of an important and polite business letter, on a mere pretext of technical formality, fails as utterly to justify his action, as does the reason of the thing.

3. Another error, Major, to which I am directed to request especial attention, consists in your entirely ignoring the fact that by General Order No. 78 of the War Department of the United States, bearing date on the 16th of September last, Major-General Butler was placed under the orders of the Governor of Massachusetts, in respect to raising, organizing, re-organizing and preparing for service any portion designed to be raised in Massachusetts, of the volunteer force which on the 10th of September he received authority from the Secretary of War to raise in the New England States.

It is not intended in this connection to raise or to discuss the question whether under existing laws the authority assumed to be granted to Major-General Butler by the War Department was not invalid from the beginning, so far as concerns the raising of troops in Massachusetts, this Commonwealth having neither refused nor omitted to respond cheerfully to every requisition for troops made upon its executive by the Federal authorities ; and the point is mentioned only to guard against the possible use of this correspondence at any future period to signify an admission on the part of the Commonwealth of Massachusetts of the right of the Federal government, under existing laws, to authorize individuals to raise troops in any State without such omission or refusal on the part of the authorities of such State to respond to requisitions.

In the present condition of National affairs, the Governor considers it impolitic and unpatriotic to embarrass the public service by undue nicety of etiquette, and he regrets that Major-General Butler's views of duty in this particular should not have corresponded with his own so as to render the present correspondence unnecessary ; but since questions of mere etiquette have thus been mooted by General Butler, I am bound by an imperative necessity which his criticism upon my letter of December 17th imposes upon me, to recall to his mind that he has himself written to Governor Andrew, without prefixing any address and without signature, and that also under circumstances which lead to the inference of intentional,—not accidental,—discourtesy, when we consider Major-General Butler's high estimate and appreciation of the forms of politeness which belong to the intercourse of officers and gentlemen.

And much less ought I in this connection, to pass unnoticed (what has never been referred to before and what would have remained without mention had not this subject of etiquette been introduced by Major-General Butler himself,) General Butler's letter of October 12th, written to Governor Andrew, but not addressed to him except in so far as he is mentioned in the third person, after the fashion of dinner invitations and the like on private and social occasions, and not signed by the Major-General with any addition of rank or command, and frequently reiterating the Governor's constitutional title and name with significant and conspicuous marks of quotation surrounding them wherever repeated.

It is customary to affix marks of quotation, in manuscript, to indicate passages or expressions borrowed from some other to whom they ought to be accredited. But I am not aware that a name given in baptism or inherited from a parent, or a title conferred by the constitution on a magistrate as his official description, are in any sense original ideas or expressions which it is usual to designate by marks of quotation. Nor is this a matter in which a gentleman of Major-General Butler's learning and urbanity could have erred by mistake. And therefore, although Governor Andrew never alluded to this circumstance, nor ever allowed it in any manner to interfere with his own courteous demeanor towards Major-General Butler in the business and correspondence of this department, yet I must now allude to it for the purpose of protesting that a matter of *purely formal* inadvertence, (*if it had been an error at all,*) committed by me in a letter addressed by the Governor's order to Major-General Butler, was not a matter to which any right remained to that officer to take exception.

When a gentleman has violated the substance of courtesy,— as did General Butler in that letter of October 12th,—by a studious, indirect, insinuating, but not less significant, intentional act of impoliteness towards a magistrate whose only offence was fidelity to his duty, to the laws, and to the rights of his official position, he cannot be permitted, without comment, to arraign another for a supposed breach of military intercourse simply formal, technical and arbitrary, as he has assumed to arraign me in this matter through yourself.

I beg, Major, that you will not consider me regardless of the exactest courtesy towards yourself, both personally, and in the official relation you sustain towards Major-General Butler; but I beg you also to excuse any undue harshness of expression, when you remember that it was by your hand that Major-General Butler repelled and criticised the letter addressed by me to him by order of my own official commander, and also that it is over your signature that he has written a letter to the Governor, making thereby an arbitrary exception to a rule which he cites against myself. The rule as he defines it, not existing, the conduct of which he complains, being strictly correct, and he being not only in an error, but in error also in the precise particular wherein he assumes to make correction, it has become my unpleasant duty to reply and in my reply to cover the whole field opened by the attack.

The whole matter concisely stated, is this: Major-General Butler recommended to Governor Andrew the appointment of certain officers to a Battery of Massachusetts Volunteer Light Artillery, just as recommendations for military appointments are daily made in great numbers to this department by individuals of every description and condition,—only that in this instance the recommendation was justly entitled to especial attention and consideration as coming from a military officer of the highest rank, for whom the Battery had been authorized by the Governor to be raised, and under whom it might be called to serve. The fact that the recommendation was communicated through an officer of Major-General Butler's staff did not change that into an official proceeding, which was necessarily and intrinsically only a personal and informal proceeding. To this recommendation the Governor directed a suitable reply to be returned by an officer of his staff, to which an answer is awaited, and His Excellency regrets that the organization of a Battery of Light Artillery already in the presence of the enemy, should be delayed by the raising at this moment of any question of etiquette, by Major-General Butler.

In conclusion, I have the honor to state that the present communication woudl be addressed to Major-General Butler personally, were His Excellency not advised by you of the absence of that officer at Washington.

I have the honor to be, Major,

Respectfully, your obedient servant,

A. G. BROWNE, Jr., *Lieut.-Col. and Military Secretary.*

ADJUTANT GENERAL'S OFFICE, WASHINGTON,
December 23, 1861.

His Excellency Governor ANDREW, *Governor of Massachusetts, Boston, Mass.*

Sir,—By direction of the Secretary of War, I enclose a list of the commissioned officers of the Eastern Bay State Regiment, under command of General Butler, with the request that you will commission the officers therein named, and, as the regiment is from your State, that you will give it a number as a Massachusetts regiment. I have the honor to request that the enclosed list may be returned to this office.

I am, Sir, very respectfully your obedient servant,

L. THOMAS, *Adjutant-General.*

ROSTER OF THE EASTERN BAY STATE REGIMENT, No. 2.

Massachusetts Volunteers, New England Division, raised by virtue of the authority of the War Department, approved by the President, Sept. 12, 1861.

FIELD.

Colonel,	———— ————, ————.
Lieutenant-Colonel,	Jonas H. French, Boston.
Major,	———— ————, ————.

STAFF.

Adjutant,	C. A. R. Dimon, Salem.
Surgeon,	Charles W. Moore, Boston.
Quartermaster,	John M. G. Parker, Dracut.
Assistant-Surgeon,	Alfred F. Holt, Cambridgeport.

NON-COMMISSIONED STAFF.

Sergeant-Major,	Selden H. Loring, Marlboro'.
Commissary-Sergeant,	Alfred F. Fay, Boston.
Quartermaster-Sergeant,	Henry W. Howe, Lowell.

Company A.

Captain,	Henry C. Welles, Cambridge.
First Lieutenant,	William G. Howe, Cambridge.
Second Lieutenant,	George F. Whitcomb, Boston.

Company B.

Captain,	Cadwallader F. Blanchard, Lowell.
First Lieutenant,	James Farsons, Lowell.
Second Lieutenant,	Edward A. Fiske, Lowell.

Company C.

Captain,	Samuel B. Shepley, Lowell.
First Lieutenant,	William F. Lovering, Lowell.
Second Lieutenant,	Richard A. Elliott, Lowell.

Company D.

Captain,	Marsh A. Ferris, Boston.
First Lieutenant,	Henry P. Fox, Boston.
Second Lieutenant,	Nathan K. Reed, Lowell.

Company E.

Captain,	———— ————, ————.
First Lieutenant,	———— ————, ————.
Second Lieutenant,	William H. Gardner, Jr., Boston.

Company F.

Captain,	Timothy A. Crowley, Lowell.
First Lieutenant,	Bart Johnson, Jr., Lowell.
Second Lieutenant,	Harrison G. Fuller, Charlestown.

Company G.

Captain,	Daniel S. Yeaton, Lawrence.
First Lieutenant,	Francis H. Whittier, Charlestown.
Second Lieutenant,	Frederic H. Norcross, Lowell.

CORRESPONDENCE.

Company H.

Captain,	Eugene A. Kelty, Boston.
First Lieutenant,	James A. Claiborne, Philadelphia, Pa.
Second Lieutenant,	Sol. Robinson, Charlestown.

Company I.

Captain,	——— ———, ———.
First Lieutenant,	——— ———, ———.
Second Lieutenant,	——— ———, ———.

Company K.

Captain,	——— ———, ———.
First Lieutenant,	——— ———, ———.
Second Lieutenant,	——— ———, ———.

HEAD-QUARTERS DEPARTMENT OF NEW ENGLAND, }
BOSTON, Dec. 20, 1861. }

The officers above named are approved by me, and recommended for commissions for their respective places. Companies I and K are recruited but not yet organized, the officers having charge of them not yet being approved.

B. F. BUTLER, *Major-General commanding*.

CAVALRY.

First Company.

Captain,	Samuel T. Reed, Attleboro', Mass.
First Lieutenant,	Jonathan E. Cowen, Fairhaven, Mass.
Second Lieutenant,	Benjamin Pickman, Salem.

Second Company.

Captain,	James M. McGee, Carlisle, Pa.
First Lieutenant,	Albert G. Bowles, Boston.
Second Lieutenant,	Pickering D. Allen, Salem.

Third Company.

Captain,	Henry A. Durivage, Waltham.
First Lieutenant,	Solon A. Perkins, Lowell.
Second Lieutenant,	Edward H. Sturtevant, Charlestown.

EXECUTIVE DEPARTMENT, BOSTON, }
December 27, 1861. }

To Brigadier General LORENZO THOMAS, *Adjutant-General U. S. Army, Washington, D. C.:*

General,—I have to acknowledge the receipt of your communication of the 23d inst. inclosing a list of names of persons entitled a " Roster of the Eastern Bay State Regiment, No. 2."

for which persons by direction of the Secretary of War you request me to issue commissions to various military grades from lieutenant-colonel to lieutenant.

I beg to suggest to you that if there is any body of troops in Massachusetts over which commissioned officers should be appointed by me, a more proper method of procedure on the part of the Secretary would be to bring that fact to my notice and to request me to issue commissions in accordance with the terms of the Act of Congress, making at the same time any recommendations according to his pleasure, instead of as in the present instance, transmitting a definite list of persons and requesting me to commission them and none other, thereby appearing to assume that the duty of the Governor of this Commonwealth in respect to commissioning officers, is only ministerial, and not discretionary and judicial in respect to the character and qualifications of persons nominated.

But passing this point entirely, and passing also the omission on the part of your communication to state that there is any body of regularly enlisted troops now in this State over whom officers should be appointed, I assume that you refer to the irregular troops which Major-General Butler has collected in the neighborhood of the city of Lowell.

By previous correspondence which I have addressed to the Secretary of War and to yourself, you are aware that these troops have been collected illegally and in contempt of orders of the war department as well as of my authority, and to the detriment and confusion of no less than ten of the volunteer regiments which have been organized by this State for the Federal service.

Nothing whatever has occurred to change my determination not to commission officers over these irregular troops since the time when that determination was first made known to Major-General Butler and to the department of war. Therefore I respectfully decline to comply with the request of the Secretary; and in examining the list of names for which commissions are requested, I recognize several as of persons who have been nominated to me for commissions in regular Massachusetts volunteer regiments, and whom I have found it not expedient to appoint.

I regret deeply that the neglect of the department of war to take action upon facts and requests presented by me in writing, in behalf of this Commonwealth, at various times since the commencement of Major-General Butler's insubordinate action, should have rendered this refusal inevitable, and should not have spared this State the confusion, division, and distress to which it has been subjected by these irregular enlistments.

It affords me equal regret to be compelled to refuse to comply with any request whatever which the war department may make upon me in the present condition of National affairs, but I find consolation in the consciousness which is confirmed by repeated assurances from the Secretary that there has never yet been any service which could properly be required of Massachusetts which has not cheerfully been rendered.

Inasmuch as the whole proceedings with reference to this irregular force collected by Major-General Butler have been conducted hitherto independently of the authority of Massachusetts, I presume that it is to be expected that they will be terminated in the same manner.

I have the honor to be, General,
Respectfully, your obedient servant,
JOHN A. ANDREW, *Governor of Massachusetts.*

EXECUTIVE DEPARTMENT, BOSTON, }
December 28, 1861. }

Honorable SIMON CAMERON, *Secretary of War, Washington, D. C.:*

My Dear Sir,—I have written to the Adjutant-General such a letter as it became my duty to write, in relation to giving commissions to the persons by him requested to command certain troops amassed in this Commonwealth by Major-General Benjamin F. Butler. But I desire in all sincerity and simplicity, to assure you, that, in spite of all the unaccountable and injurious conduct of that gentleman, against which I have remonstrated in vain, I am still anxious that the public service, in the interest of which I have all along acted, should be promoted even by the organization of that force, if such is the wish of the government, and if it can be done in some manner consistent with propriety and the welfare of the corps itself. If the government wishes me to organize those men into companies and a regiment, and to appoint and commission officers, and shall so request, difficult and thankless as will be the task, I will nevertheless undertake it. I shall, of course, receive and pay the respect to any recommendations of Major-General Butler, due to his rank and position. But I must frankly say that there are men whose names, I perceive, are likely to be proposed to me, and on which I presume General Butler is likely to insist, whom I could not in conscience appoint, and whom to commission would offend both my sense of honor and of duty.

There is nothing a just and honest man can do, which I do not feel a conscious willingness to attempt, nothing an honorable mind can bear, I do not feel willing to endure, to serve the country and her cause, and to obey the wishes of the administration. In all these military matters I regard myself a servant, though with some discretionary powers; and in the sphere of my proper subordination, obedience is my pleasure as well as my duty; but in the sphere of my proper and lawful discretion, although limited and inferior, I must still use my own discretion, cautiously and respectfully, I grant, but yet with firmness and fidelity.

I am, with great respect, your friend and servant,
JOHN A. ANDREW.

HEAD-QUARTERS, DEPARTMENT OF NEW ENGLAND,
BOSTON, Dec. 28, 1861.

His Excellency JOHN A. ANDREW, *Governor:*

On my return home, at the earliest possible moment, I reply in person to your note, in the character of a citizen.

The official reply, sent by Major Strong, I approve and ordered, as covering the points upon which I believed a discourtesy had been done by your Military Secretary, with whom personally, for reasons appearing to me sufficient, I had refused to hold farther correspondence.

I have read the letter in reply from your Military Secretary, and do not propose to reply to it at length.

Having enrolled yourself, by your own act, in the "United States Army of Massachusetts Volunteers," the evidence of which I send herewith, I thought it at least no discourtesy to treat you as my equal in the assimulated rank, which could be given you by courtesy only, especially in a correspondence upon military matters, and to ask of you a like courtesy. You will not, certainly, take the public and published honors of enrolment in the United States Army of Massachusetts Volunteers without incurring the corresponding obligations of courtesy and responsibility; and while I never supposed that, for any violations of regulations of the War Department, the Governor of Massachusetts could be deposed, yet I do believe that, for such violations, he will be likely to have his assumptions of command of those volunteers, either at home or on the lines of the Potomac, signally rebuked. Of this, I believe, you have had some experience.

I shall not notice, further, either the matter or the manner of that note, save to say that I disclaim, most emphatically, any intentional or even accidental discourtesy to the Governor of Massachusetts.

I have by far too high a respect for the office to wish to aid in lowering its dignity.

In the matter of the address in quotation, I but copied the address assumed by one of the numerous military secretaries who write me on behalf of the Governor, and it was because of the formality of that address, "His Excellency Governor Andrew" is neither a "baptismal, inherited or constitutional" title, and after using it once in the letter alluded to, I carefully used the title of the Constitution, and marked it in quotation, to call attention to the difference.

I was the more careful to use the third person in the letter, because I was asking a favorable consideration to a request, and in that case I am not taught to sign the rank with which I have been honored. The Major-Generals of the United States seldom officially ask favors. You will also observe that therein I used the third person in speaking of myself.

May I call your attention to the fact that the rules in regard to *set-off*, used in the profession which we both practiced, and which, perhaps, it would have been better for both and for the country if we had never left, do not apply to the courtesies of life. If you have, by accident, treated me discourteously, it is no set-off that I had accidentally, or even intentionally, treated you discourteously. As soon as it is thus made such set-off, then your discourtesy becomes *intentional*. But something too much of all this. As you have disclaimed all intentional discourtesy, that is sufficient. If my attention had been called to any supposed want of courtesy on my part, I should have at once disclaimed it, as I now do. Let, then, the citizen speak to the citizen, and say, without circumlocution, paraphrase or euphuism, that in the matter of the officers of the Light Battery, I should not have recommended Captain Manning unless I had supposed that he was specially desired by yourself and the Adjutant-General. If he does not commend himself to you, I have no objection to his not being commissioned, and will offer another. With regard to the other officers, their good conduct, after several weeks' trial, commended them both to me and their men. If any base charge can be substantiated against either of them, I shall be happy to substitute others; I believe, however, that neither of them have ever done any thing worse than seducing a mother, and making a father wifeless, and children motherless; and that, you know, is no objection to a high military commission in Massachusetts. I believe neither of them dead or physically disabled, as suggested in your note. If apology is needed for not notifying you of the fact that the Battery was going to sea, I must say that your supposed absence from the Commonwealth during all the time from the organization of the company till the exigencies of the service required them to go, is the best that I can offer.

They had been ordered to report to me; were under my control; had been mustered into the service of the United States; and with their future movements, I respectfully submit, you had nothing to do, save to give commissions, if you so choose. If not, it is but justice to these men so to say. You have stated that this Battery sailed "incompletely uniformed and equipped, and not fully recruited;" *that* is fully denied, and you must have been misinformed.

CORRESPONDENCE.

Enclosed is the evidence of your voluntary enrolment into the United States Army of Massachusetts Volunteers.

I am, most respectfully,
Your fellow-citizen,
BENJ. F. BUTLER.

[Accompanying the letter of which the foregoing is a copy, was forwarded a newspaper entitled, "*New England Meridian*, News, Literature, Politics, Science, and General Information, Vol. I., No. 3. Boston, December 21, 1861;" on the fifth page of which newspaper was marked in ink a printed roster of the general and personal staff of the commander-in-chief of the Massachusetts Militia, underneath the heading "United States Army Roll of Massachusetts Volunteers," and written in ink upon the margin of the newspaper opposite this roster is the following:—

"I certify that this publication, while in proof, was submitted to Governor Andrew, and approved by him in its present form.
J. B. MANSFIELD, *Editor.*
Dec. 29, 1861.
A true copy.
JOS. M. BELL, *A. A. D. C.*"

Upon this newspaper, as it is now placed upon the files of the executive department, is written further the following endorsement:—

"*Memorandum.*—This list of names was shown to me one day in the doric hall of the State House, by a gentleman purporting to be engaged on a book. He stated that he desired me to sit for a likeness to be inserted in the book, and requested me to do him the favor to correct any errors in the list. I looked it over with what care I could, and corrected some errors which I noticed; but I did not comply with the remaining request. I never saw the newspaper until General Butler sent it to me, and I have no memory of the heading which seems to have misled that gentleman. The list is a roster containing the names of the commander-in-chief of the militia of Massachusetts and the members of his general and personal staff, no one of whom belonged to the United States Volunteers. J. A. A."]

EXECUTIVE DEPARTMENT, BOSTON,
January 1, 1862.

Adjutant-General WILLIAM SCHOULER:

In the matter of the Fourth Battery, which marched by order of Major-General Butler, not having had its officers appointed or commissioned, but for which company certain officers are recommended by Major Strong, representing General Butler, as being the choice of the company, I have to request that commissions be filled out accordingly. If the subject had been properly brought to my attention in due season, it would have enabled me to consult the best interests of the corps by selecting from whatever source the best candidates offering. As it is, the Battery being in the field, at a very remote point, and under these persons as acting officers, trusting that their superior commander will look after its interests, since I cannot, under the existing difficulties of investigation, pass any perfectly satisfactory judgment on all of them, I have decided to assume that commissions had best be granted, and to approve the recommendation of Major Strong,—this being, as I understand, your own opinion and advice.

Yours respectfully,

JOHN A. ANDREW.

EXECUTIVE DEPARTMENT, BOSTON,
December 30, 1861.

To Major-General B. F. BUTLER, &c., &c., &c.:

Sir,—It becomes my duty to ask you to what officer or appointment you refer in your letter of the 28th instant, in using the following words, viz.:—

"Seducing a mother, and making a father wifeless, and children motherless; and that, you know, is no objection to a high military commission in Massachusetts."

Moreover, may I ask whose mother is alluded to, and whose wife; and does the implied allegation mean that the crime of murder was added to that of seduction; although the words "you know," assume the existence of greater knowledge than I possess. And, indeed, since the day I had the honor to detail yourself as a Brigadier-General of militia, at the beginning of the present war, to this day, and both inclusive, I cannot accuse myself of such an appointment. If I have done so, I beg you to expose it.

I have the honor to be your obedient,
JOHN A. ANDREW.

HEAD-QUARTERS, DEPARTMENT OF NEW ENGLAND,
BOSTON, January 1, 1862.

To His Excellency, JOHN A. ANDREW, *Governor:*

At the earliest possible moment of relief from graver duties, I answer your Excellency's communication of the 30th ult. I referred in my communication of the 28th ult., to the case of Wyman, appointed by your Excellency, Colonel of the 16th Massachusetts Regiment.

Unless the testimony of brother officers serving with Wyman is to be disbelieved, facts notorious are to be denied which have never been denied before.

Col. Wyman while an officer in the United States Army held long adulterous intercourse with a Mrs. Brannon, a wife of a brother officer.

This woman afterwards left her home under such circumstances as to induce the belief that she was either murdered by herself or another.

This Wyman obtained leave of absence from the Army, and joined his paramour in Europe. While there, he resigned his commission because of a letter from the Adjutant-General of the Army that he would be court martialed if he did not, and remained abroad until after the breaking out of the war, when he left her embraces and returned to the arms of the Commonwealth under your Excellency's appointment.

This woman was the mother of children, and if I should amend the language of my communication of the 28th ult., I should add, " making a father worse than wifeless, and children worse than motherless."

I used the phrase " you know," because I have been informed, and I have reason to believe and do believe that the substance of these facts was known to your Excellency at the time you made the appointment.

Will your Excellency deny that you were then put upon inquiry as to them?

I cannot expose this matter, because it has long since been made a matter of exposition in the public prints.

I have no farther knowledge of Colonel Wyman save that which may be learned by inquiry of any officer of the Army who served with him.

I have no disposition to injure or interfere with him, and have made this communication only in reply to your Excellency's statement.

I remain, very respectfully,
Your Excellency's obedient servant,
BENJ. F. BUTLER.

EXECUTIVE DEPARTMENT, BOSTON,
January 6, 1862.

Major-General BENJAMIN F. BUTLER, &c., &c., &c.:

Sir,—At the first hour at my disposal for the purpose I acknowledge the receipt of your letter of January 1st in which you state that Colonel Powell T. Wyman, commanding the 16th Regiment Massachusetts Volunteer Infantry, now stationed at Fortress Monroe, is the person to whom you had reference when addressing me under date of December 28th you asserted that I "know" that "seducing a mother, and making a father wifeless and children motherless," "is no objection to a high military commission in Massachusetts."

In answer to your somewhat peremptory interrogatory addressed to me in that letter of January 1st, I would state for your information that the first knowledge I ever had of Mr. Wyman was through a letter addressed by him to the Adjutant-General of Massachusetts, dated "London, England, May 1, 1861," stating that he was a citizen of Boston, and a graduate of the West Point Military Academy, and had served for ten years as an officer of artillery of the United States Army; and tendering his services to the Executive of this

Commonwealth, in any military capacity. I am not aware that any acknowledgment was ever made of this communication.

During the month of June I received another note from Mr. Wyman, dated at the Parker House, Boston, he having in the meanwhile returned to America. This letter was assigned to a member of my staff to whom Mr. Wyman was referred for consultation. It was at that time that I first heard that there was said to be a cloud of some sort upon Mr. Wyman's character; and having little leisure myself to enter into quasi-judicial investigations as to personal character, I passed over his name in the appointments which I then was making. The nature of the reports against him were not then stated to me, and although I was soon after advised of them, yet there are things asserted in your letter of January 1st as "notorious facts" of which it is only through yourself that I have knowledge.

Very shortly afterwards Adam W. Thaxter, Esq., of this city,—doubtless known to you as one of the most distinguished merchants of Boston,—brought the name of Mr. Wyman very urgently to my attention, both personally and in a letter dated June 20th, in which he requested me to call on himself if Mr. Wyman should "need an endorser," and stated that in his opinion Mr. Wyman, if appointed a Colonel, would "do credit to his native State."

And on July 1st, Mr. Thaxter further presented to me a communication in writing, signed by Captain Thomas J. C. Amory, of the 7th Infantry United States Army, and Captain Louis H. Marshall, of the 10th Infantry, United States Army, both of whom had served in the army with Mr. Wyman, and who were, if I remember, the only United States regular army officers then on duty at this city; and signed also by Charles G. Greene, Esq., Franklin Haven, Esq., William Dehon, Esq., William Parkman, Esq., Hon. George Lunt, Hon. Benjamin F. Hallett, Henry L. Hallett, Esq., P. Holmes, Esq., Edward F. Bradlee, Esq., Joseph L. Henshaw, Esq., Peter Butler, Esq., Thomas C. Amory, Esq., and J. P. Bradlee, Esq.,—all of these, gentlemen of this city, who are doubtless known to you by reputation, and with some of whom I cannot doubt that you are personally acquainted,—in which communication these gentlemen requested the appointment of Mr. Wyman as a Colonel, and certified that they "believed in him" as "a gentleman, a man of worth, an accomplished officer, and brave soldier, and that a regiment under his command would yield to none in the service for discipline, high tone, and efficiency," and also that they felt convinced that "under all circumstances" he "would do honor to his State and to his Country." These gentlemen further stated that they made this request in full knowledge of the existence of the rumors and influences against Mr. Wyman's reputation; and, nevertheless, with such knowledge, they earnestly "urged" him "as one to whom the honor of Massachusetts may confidently be trusted."

About the same time Mr. Wyman addressed to me a communication in writing, denying the truth of the prejudicial rumors in circulation against him, and although admitting that it was true that he had formed a matrimonial connection with a lady who had eloped from her husband by reason of that husband's brutal treatment of her, yet stating also that he had not seen the lady for the year preceding, nor for the year after her elopement. This communication, I find, upon referring to it, amounts also to a denial of the truth of much that is stated by you in your letter of January 1st, as "notorious facts" derogatory to Mr. Wyman's character.

Upon the basis of this statement made by Mr. Wyman, and controlled by no responsible counter-statement or testimony whatsoever, and upon the formal assurance I received from the numerous gentlemen whom I have mentioned, that he was a good soldier, and a good citizen, I did not feel myself justified in rejecting the services of a highly meritorious and thoroughly educated officer, upon unsubstantial rumors of an alleged moral error which did not affect his military competency,—and more especially at a time when the services of educated officers were so greatly needed for the command of our troops.

I therefore appointed Mr. Wyman to be Colonel of the 16th Regiment, an appointment which under the circumstances stated, commended itself to my judgment, and which I have no reason whatsoever now to regret, and under like circumstances, should not hesitate to repeat.

As it was upon the faith of the assurances made to me by Mr. Thaxter and the other gentlemen in their communication of July 1st, that the appointment of Colonel Wyman was made, I therefore conceive that your quarrel with that appointment should be with those gentlemen rather than with myself, and therefore I propose to inclose copies of your correspondence with me in this connection, to Mr. Thaxter as representing them, and I must request you to address to them any future correspondence upon this subject, inasmuch as they are better acquainted than myself with Colonel Wyman and his character, life, and connections, which I know chiefly through them. I desire to add that in all the intercourse which I have had with Colonel Wyman during the organization of his regiment, I never observed on his part the manifestation of any other qualities than those of an accomplished officer, and I shall be very reluctant to give credit to your reproaches against his character, especially in view of the standing of those gentlemen by whom his character as a gentleman was certified to me.

In conclusion, I would say that I do not feel that any reason exists, *requiring* me to enter into such an explanation as the above; but when an officer of the rank of Major-General in the Army of United States Volunteers, thinks it necessary to diversify his occupations by needless flings at a fellow officer in the same army,—seeking to strike *myself* through *him*,—a sense of honor and duty both to the Commonwealth and to the gentleman thus struck at, requires me to spare no proper pains to see that justice is fully done.

Your obedient servant,

JOHN A. ANDREW.

ADJUTANT-GENERAL'S OFFICE, WASHINGTON,
January 3, 1862.

His Excellency, the Governor of Massachusetts, Boston, Massachusetts.

Governor,—The Secretary of War requests that you will forward to this office, at your earliest convenience, a return of the two and three years regiments, and independent companies furnished up to this date, under the authority of your State,—setting forth the strength of each regiment or independent company, and the respective arms to which they belonged when transferred to the General Government. He further desires that you will forward a similar return (or as complete a one as it may be in your power to render,) of all two or three years volunteer troops raised within the limits of your State upon what has been termed "independent acceptances." He also requests that you will report the number of regiments or independent companies now organizing in your State, the present strength thereof, and the time at which they will probably be completed and ready to take the field.

I am, Governor, very respectfully,
Your obedient servant,
L. THOMAS, *Adjutant-General.*

EXECUTIVE DEPARTMENT, BOSTON,
January 9, 1862.

To Brigadier-General LORENZO THOMAS, *Adjutant-General, U. S. Army, Washington, D. C.:*

General,—His Excellency Governor Andrew, has to acknowledge the receipt of your letter of the 3d instant, in which you request to be informed:—

1. The number of regiments of two years volunteers; also, of three years volunteers; and also the number of independent companies of volunteers furnished by Massachusetts, to the date of your communication.

2. The strength of each regiment or company, and 3. The arm of the service to which each belonged when transferred to the General Government.

4. Similar details as to all two or three years volunteer troops raised within the limits of Massachusetts upon what has been termed "independent acceptances."

5. The number of regiments or independent companies now organizing in Massachusetts, the present strength thereof, and the time at which they will probably be completed and ready to take the field.

The answers to these inquiries will be found in the statements hereto annexed.

I have the honor to be, respectfully,
Your obedient servant,
A. G. BROWNE, Jr.,
Lieut.-Colonel and Military Secretary.

Statement annexed to Reply of January 9th, to the Letter of Adjutant-General Thomas of January 3, 1862.

Question 1.—The number of regiments of two years volunteers? *Answer.*—None.

——The number of regiment of three years volunteers?
A.—Twenty-five. (24 of infantry, 1 of cavalry.)

——The number of independent companies of volunteers?
A.—Five, (of infantry,) battalion at Fort Warren. Six, (of infantry,) serving in New York regiments, four of them in what is called the Mozart Regiment, and two in what is called the Excelsior Brigade. One (of infantry) forming part of the garrison at Fortress Monroe. Five (of light artillery,) battery companies. Two, (of sharpshooters). Making a total of twenty-four regiments and twelve companies, of infantry, one regiment of cavalry, two companies of sharpshooters and five batteries of light artillery.

Questions 2 and 3.—The strength of each regiment or company when transferred to the General Government, and the arm of the service to which each then belonged.

Answer.—

INFANTRY.*

No. of Regiment.	Strength when transferred to Gen'l Gov'm't.
First,	1,120
Second,	1,072
Seventh,	1,043
Ninth,	1,067
Tenth,	1,045
Eleventh,	1,055
Twelfth,	1,058
Thirteenth,	1,038
Fourteenth,	1,015
Fifteenth,	1,137

* It will be noticed that in numbering the infantry regiments the numbers Three, Four, Five, Six, and Eight, have been omitted, those having been the numbers of the *militia* regiments furnished by this State to the General Government in April for three months service.

Sixteenth,	1,061
Seventeenth,	1,003
Eighteenth,	996
Nineteenth,	926
Twentieth,	757
Twenty-First,	958
Twenty-Second,	1,033
Twenty-Third,	1,004
Twenty-Fourth,	975
Twenty-Fifth,	1,025
Twenty-Sixth,	1,040
Twenty-Seventh,	958
Twenty-Eighth,*	945
Twenty-Ninth,	808
Battalion at Fort Warren,	476
Company at Fort Munroe,	98
Six companies in New York regiments,	500
Total of Infantry,	25,246

CAVALRY.

First Regiment,	1,101
Total of Cavalry,	1,101

ARTILLERY.

Light Batteries—

First,	150
Second,	157
Third,	155
Fourth,†	157
Fifth,	156
Total of Artillery,	775

* In the table of Infantry, the present strength of the Twenty-Eighth Regiment is given, and that regiment is enumerated as if it had already left the State, it being under orders to leave on Saturday next, and proceed to Fort Columbus, New York, and there report to Colonel Loomis, United States Army, commanding.

† In the table of Artillery, the strength of the Fourth Battery is computed from observation, and from unofficial papers; that Battery having been removed from this State by Major-General Butler, without any notice being given to the Governor, without any officers having been commissioned, and without any proper rolls of any description having been deposited in the office of the Adjutant-General of the Commonwealth, of which facts the Adjutant-General of the United States Army was advised by the Governor under date of November 27th.

Besides the troops thus above enumerated, it is estimated that upwards of two thousand men have been enlisted from Massachusetts chiefly into New York Regiments, of whom about 300 are in what is called the Union Coast Guard Regiment now at Fortress Monroe.

SHARPSHOOTERS.

Companies—
    First, .   102
    Second,   104

       Total of Sharpshooters, .   206

SUMMARY.

	Strength.
Infantry, 24 Regiments and 12 Companies, .	25,246
Cavalry, 1 Regiment, ...	1,101
Artillery, 5 Battery Companies, . . .	775
Sharpshooters, 2 Companies, . . .	206
Grand total, .	27,328

Question 4.—Similar details as to "all two or three years volunteer troops raised within the limits of Massachusetts upon what has been termed 'independent acceptances.'"

Answer.—Prior to September 16, 1861, which was the date of General Order, No. 78, of the War Department of the United States, for the past year, all attempts to raise troops in this State by individuals on what you style "independent acceptances" proved abortive, and there are no corps now in the field which were raised in this State under any other superintendence than that of the State government.

But since the date of that Order, Major-General Butler United States Volunteers, in violation of its provisions, has collected an irregular force, in camps at Pittsfield and Lowell, which according to the best information in the Governor's possession, is believed to amount to about 1,800 men at this time. Part of these men have been confined during the last week on board the steamer Constitution lying in Boston Harbor, under Major-General Butler's orders. No data are in the possession of the State Government for furnishing officially, or any more accurately, the number or position of the irregular force thus illegally collected; as the whole business of collecting it, has been conducted independently of, and in contempt of the authority of this Commonwealth, and of the Order of the War Department before mentioned (No. 78) and no report has ever been made by Major-General Butler to the Governor of this State as required and commanded by that Order.

Full representations of these facts have been made to the War Department, and may be found by referring to letters addressed to the Secretary of War under dates of October 6th, and December 28th, and to yourself under dates of November 27th, and December 27th.

Question 5.—"The number of regiments or independent companies now organizing in Massachusetts, the present strength thereof, and the time at which they will probably be completed, and ready to take the field."

Answer.—It is impossible to state with any approach to accuracy, the condition, in respect to the points of the above inquiry, of the irregular bodies of troops illegally assembled by Major-General Butler, any further than is set forth in the answer to interrogatory No. 4.

The Twenty-Eighth Infantry Regiment is the only one of the regiments raised under the superintendence of the authorities of Massachusetts which still remains in this Commonwealth, and that regiment, as appears by the answer to questions number 2 and 3, is now 945 strong, and is under orders to leave the Commonwealth for Fort Columbus, New York, on Saturday, the eleventh inst.

By General Order, No. 105 of the War Department of the United States, of the series of the past year, issued on December 3, 1861, it was provided that "no more regiments, batteries or independent companies will be raised by the Governors of the States except upon the special requisition of the War Department." No such requisition has since that date been received by the Governor of this Commonwealth.

The Twenty-Eighth Infantry Regiment, before mentioned, is the only corps of volunteers which at that date was in process of organization by the authorities of Massachusetts, which has not already left the State. At the time of the receipt of that Order of December third, the Governor of Massachusetts had received from the War Department assurances that four additional regiments to those which appear in the schedules of the answers to questions 2 and 3 would be accepted from the authorities of this Commonwealth; but no definite action had been taken to initiate their organization, inasmuch as before proceeding to raise any further troops, the Governor awaited the response of the War Department to his request to be relieved from the irregular and illegal competition instituted by Major-General Butler. The courtesy of such a response is still awaited by the Executive of this Commonwealth; and the delay is the more to be regretted inasmuch as preparations had then been completed by the authorities of Massachusetts, for the organization in Worcester, Franklin, Hampshire,

Hampden and Berkshire Counties, of a regiment of admirable material, (to be commanded by D. Waldo Lincoln, Esq., the son of ex-Governor Levi Lincoln of Worcester,) as one of the four remaining to be organized. It will be inexpedient to attempt the organization of any further regiments in this State under the authority of the Commonwealth, so long as the Department of War permits Major-General Butler to persist in his present course of action, which prevented Massachusetts from participation in the expedition to Port Royal in the manner she had expected, and others had expected of her, which has retarded and confused the enlistments of no less than ten of the regiments of the State, and which has demoralized the entire recruiting service in this portion of the country.

[Telegram.]
WASHINGTON, D. C., January 11, 1862.

Governor JOHN A. ANDREW, *Boston:*

I will be greatly obliged if you will arrange somehow with General Butler to officer his two unofficered regiments.

A. LINCOLN.

EXECUTIVE DEPARTMENT, BOSTON, }
January 11, 1862. }

To the President of the United States:

Sir,—I have the honor to acknowledge the receipt of your telegram of to-day, stating your desire that some arrangement shall be made by which I may organize with officers the troops which have been illegally collected in this State, by Major-General Butler; and, in reply, I beg to repeat what I wrote to the Secretary of War, on December 28th, that if the Federal Government wishes me to organize these men into companies and regiments, and to appoint and commission officers, and shall so request and issue orders accordingly, difficult and thankless as will be the task, I will, nevertheless, undertake it, and I should pay the respect to any recommendations of Major-General Butler due to his rank and position. But I must frankly say that there are names which I perceive he would be likely to propose to me, of persons whom I could not in conscience appoint, and whom to commission would offend both my sense of honor and of duty.

In the sphere of my proper subordination, obedience is my pleasure as well as my duty, but in the sphere of my proper and lawful discretion, although limited and inferior, I must use such discretion cautiously and respectfully, but with firmness and fidelity; and the choice of officers is a duty not simply ministerial, but discretionary and judicial as to their character and qualifications.

Major-General Butler's proceedings in Massachusetts, in respect to recruitment, have been altogether lawless, in violation, especially, of General Order No. 78 of the War Department, of the series of 1861, and have been conducted with both official and personal contempt towards the Government of this Commonwealth.

This has been permitted by the General Government, notwithstanding representations of the facts to the Adjutant-General of the Army, and to the Secretary of War, for which I beg to refer you to the files of the War Department, mentioning especially my letters to the Secretary, of October 6th and December 28th, and to the Adjutant-General of November 27th and December 27th.

In an ordinary time, such insult by an officer of the Federal Government, and such neglect by that Government to check its continuance or prevent its repetition, would have demanded public remonstrance. In a time like this, it is the duty of every citizen to bear whatever can be borne consistently with honor, and I have been silent towards the public, trusting that the Federal Government would at last discontinue the toleration of this indignity, practiced towards a Commonwealth which had done nothing to deserve it; and in that trust I remain silent still.

If you desire more particular details of the action of Major-General Butler relative to the Government of Massachusetts, and to his recruitment in this State, I respectfully refer you to the Senators of Massachusetts in Congress, and to copies of correspondence and documents relating to the subject, which are in their possession.

In my opinion, which I submit with entire respect, there is no necessity for the organization at all of the men whom General Butler has thus collected, and who are, as you state, unofficered. They cannot be required for immediate service under his command, for the 28th Regiment of our Massachusetts line, which (together with our 26th) I raised for him and placed at his disposal, has, after being fully recruited and equipped, been ordered to leave the State for entirely another service. They cannot render any more effectual benefit to the country than by being used to recruit to the maximum standard the Massachusetts regiments already in the field, and particularly the 15th and 20th, which were more than decimated at Ball's Bluff, and the recruitment for which has been checked and embarrassed by the insubordinate competition of General Butler. This also would admit their needy families to the benefits of the State law for the relief of the needy families of soldiers in regular Massachusetts regiments.

But if, on the contrary, the Federal Government shall deem it more beneficent to the public service, that these men should be organized into companies and regiments and by the appointment of officers, and shall request me to undertake that duty in the manner in which I have performed it in the instances of the twenty-five regiments which this State has hitherto contributed to the army, exercising my own discretion in all matters in the same manner as with those twenty-five regiments, I will assume the task and perform it according to my best judgment and ability,—and to that end, Major-General Butler should be directed to report in accordance with the General Order, No. 78, and otherwise to comply with the provisions of that Order, which as yet he has entirely neglected and disobeyed.

In event of the Federal Government requesting me to undertake the organization of these men, I should be pleased to hear more definitely from the Secretary of War, with reference to the employment in Massachusetts regiments of some of the foreign officers now tendering their services to the United States, on which subject he has already addressed me. If there are such officers, of marked merit, for whom other commands have not been secured, it would be possible to issue commissions to some of them, if adequate reasons should appear for their employment in accordance with the request of the Secretary.

I have the honor to be, with the highest respect,
Your obedient servant,

JOHN A. ANDREW.

[Telegram.]

WASHINGTON, D. C., January 15, 1862.

To the Governor of Massachusetts, Boston:

What number of troops can you have ready, fully equipped, for marching within one week from this date?

THOMAS A. SCOTT, *Ass't. Sec'y of War.*

[Telegram.]

EXECUTIVE DEPARTMENT, BOSTON,
January 17, 1862.

Col. THOMAS A. SCOTT, *Ass't. Sec'y of War, Washington, D. C.:*

Your telegram is just received. Please read communication to Adjutant-General Thomas of January 9th. The proceedings of General Butler prevented us from starting new regiments authorized; and the new army orders have taken every thing out of my hands. I will do every thing possible for the government if called on, *and the orders adhered to.*

JOHN A. ANDREW.

[On December 21st, 1861, copies of all the foregoing letters and documents to that date were forwarded to the Senators of Massachusetts in the Congress of the United States, as follows:]

EXECUTIVE DEPARTMENT, BOSTON,
December 21, 1861.

To Honorable CHARLES SUMNER, and
Honorable HENRY WILSON:

Senators,—I appeal to you as the official representatives of this Commonwealth in the Congress of the United States, and its proper agents at the seat of government, to examine, and in your official capacity to act upon the official copies of correspondence which I have the honor herewith to inclose, by presenting the subject formally to the President of the United States.

For an immediate comprehension of its purport I would suggest to you before examining the file consecutively, to read—
1. My letter to Adjutant-General Thomas, under date of November 27th.
2. The letter addressed by me to the Secretary of War, under date of October 6th.
3. The letters addressed to Major-General Butler on October 5th and October 26th.

The other documents explain, illustrate, and fortify the facts stated and positions assumed in these letters.

As I do not receive any reply from the officers of the Federal Government whom I have thus addressed, nor any redress, or cessation of the evils of which complaint is therein made, I am compelled thus to resort to your official intervention.

It is not my judgment that this Commonwealth is properly subject either to open injustice or to contemptuous silence. I do not think that the people of Massachusetts can endure that I should fail to fully assert their rights and vindicate their interests although obliged to do so in connection with the upholding of my own official functions.

However humble and unimportant may be the person, individually, who happens at this time to hold the place of the Chief Executive Magistrate of Massachusetts, is not to be remembered by you or by himself. But when the venerable Commonwealth which he serves, is thus treated with contumely, although in his own person, it is not permitted even to him to remain silent.

Perhaps the blood shed by the children of this Commonwealth at Baltimore, at Ball's Bluff, and wherever else they have been called in arms during the present year, may have been only their dutiful share in the sufferings of the war; but it is neither in my heart nor in my temper to see the public service injured, our people distracted, and our military efficiency demoralized by proceedings at once unjust and discourteous to the truest friend the Federal Government and its administration have found among all the States in this hour of their trial, and the best blood of whose sons has been freely poured out upon every field.

Since I can obtain no word of reply to myself in answer to the representations and requests made in these letters, I trust that you may be more fortunate.

I am compelled to declare, with great reluctance and regret, that the whole course of proceeding under Major-General Butler in this Commonwealth seems to have been designed and adapted simply to afford means to persons of bad character to make money unscrupulously, and to encourage men whose unfitness had excluded them from any appointment by me to the volunteer military service, to hope for such appointment over Massachusetts troops, from other authority than that of the Executive of Massachusetts.

I am, very respectfully,
Your most obedient and humble servant,
JOHN A. ANDREW, *Governor of Massachusetts.*

Besides an acknowledgment of the receipt of the letter of December 21st and its inclosures, the reply following (which was received on January 14, 1862,) was returned :—

WASHINGTON, D. C., Jan. 10, 1862.

I am authorized by the War Department to say that if you will send on your programme, with reference to General Butler, it shall be carried out and the Department given up. Please let me know your desires.

CHARLES SUMNER.

To Governor ANDREW.

[Telegram.]
EXECUTIVE DEPARTMENT, BOSTON,
January 14, 1862.

Hon. CHARLES SUMNER, *U. S. Senator, Washington, D. C.:*

The President has my programme written, replying to his telegram of last Saturday. My letters should be *directly* and not *indirectly* answered by the President or Department.

JOHN A. ANDREW.

www.ingramcontent.com/pod-product-compliance
Lightning Source LLC
Chambersburg PA
CBHW020308090426
42735CB00009B/1261